AFRICAN AMERICAN

The Complete Guide to Writing

Effective and

Award-Winning

Business Proposals

Step-by-Step Instructions

By Jean Murray

The Complete Guide to Writing Effective & Award-Winning Business Proposals: Step-by-Step Instructions

ISBN-13: 978-1-60138-234-4   ISBN-10: 1-60138-234-0

Library of Congress Cataloging-in-Publication Data

Murray, Jean Wilson.
  The complete guide to writing effective and award winning business proposals : step-by-step instructions / by Jean Wilson Murray.
    p. cm.
Includes bibliographical references and index.
ISBN-13: 978-1-60138-234-4 (alk. paper)
ISBN-10: 1-60138-234-0 (alk. paper)
1. Proposal writing in business. 2. Business report writing. I. Title.

HF5718.5.M86 2008
658.15'224--dc22
                          2008015499

INTERIOR LAYOUT DESIGN: Nicole Deck ndeck@atlantic-pub.com

Printed in the United States

Printed on Recycled Paper

DEDICATION

To my parents

We recently lost our beloved pet, Bear, who was not only our best and dearest friend, but also the "Vice President of Sunshine" here at Atlantic Publishing. He did not receive a salary but worked tirelessly 24 hours a day to please his parents. Bear was a rescue dog who turned around and showered myself, my wife Sherri, his grandparents Jean, Bob and Nancy, and every person and animal he met (maybe not rabbits) with friendship and love. He made a lot of people smile every day.

We wanted you to know that a portion of the profits of this book will be donated to the Humane Society of the United States.

–Douglas & Sherri Brown

THE HUMANE SOCIETY
OF THE UNITED STATES©

The human-animal bond is as old as human history. We cherish our animal companions for their unconditional affection and acceptance. We feel a thrill when we glimpse wild creatures in their natural habitat or in our own backyard.

Unfortunately, the human-animal bond has at times been weakened. Humans have exploited some animal species to the point of extinction.

The Humane Society of the United States makes a difference in the lives of animals here at home and worldwide. The HSUS is dedicated to creating a world where our relationship with animals is guided by compassion. We seek a truly humane society in which animals are respected for their intrinsic value, and where the human-animal bond is strong.

Want to help animals? We have plenty of suggestions. Adopt a pet from a local shelter, join the Humane Society and be a part of our work to help companion animals and wildlife. You will be funding our educational, legislative, investigative and outreach projects in the U.S. and across the globe.

Or perhaps you'd like to make a memorial donation in honor of a pet, friend or relative? You can through our Kindred Spirits program. And if you'd like to contribute in a more structured way, our Planned Giving Office has suggestions about estate planning, annuities, and even gifts of stock that avoid capital gains taxes.

Maybe you have land that you would like to preserve as a lasting habitat for wildlife. Our Wildlife Land Trust can help you. Perhaps the land you want to share is a backyard—that's enough. Our Urban Wildlife Sanctuary Program will show you how to create a habitat for your wild neighbors.

So you see, it's easy to help animals. And the HSUS is here to help.

The Humane Society of the United States
2100 L Street NW
Washington, DC 20037
202-452-1100
www.hsus.org

TABLE OF CONTENTS

Introduction

Business people write proposals for a number of purposes, including, but not limited to:

- To obtain loans from banks, lenders, and investors

- To sell products to customers

- To sell their professional services to clients

- To persuade their bosses to undertake a new project

As a professional in business, whether you are a small single-owner business or a large multinational firm, you will likely be called upon at one time or another in your career to write a business proposal or two.

Like most business endeavors, writing your first business proposal entails a steep learning curve. There are many things to think about, including the general format and sections, the result you want to achieve, and the audience for which you are writing. If you have never written a business proposal before, you may be tempted to purchase an expensive business proposal template or business proposal software. If you do, you will find the template or software only gives you an outline. You will still need to answer questions like these:

- Who is my audience and what do they want?

- What do I need to do to enhance my credibility with this audience?

- How can I effectively present my case so the audience will respond positively to my proposal?

- What writing style should I use?

- How should I include references, demographics, statistics, and other data?

- How can I modify this template to fit my specific case?

In this book, I present a complete guide to writing effective and award-winning business proposals. An "effective" business proposal will achieve the result you want and an "award-winning" business proposal will bring you the reward you want, whether it is a monetary or personal one.

The process of preparing a business proposal has three phases: preparation, writing, and presentation. The preparation phase is the most important; if you plan your proposal carefully and think about what you want to say and how you want to say it, you will find it easier to write and to make your message meaningful. The writing phase is where you put down the information and ideas you have gathered in the planning phase, and where you construct your award-winning proposal. The presentation phase involves using visuals and PowerPoint slides effectively.

To mirror these three phases, this book is divided into three sections: Planning, Writing, and Presentation. In the Planning section, you will go through the process of planning your business proposal, including discussions relating to:

- Understanding your audience

- Creating a value proposition for the client

- Key elements of the successful business proposal

- The elements of effective business writing

- Avoiding writing problems and ethical dilemmas in the writing process

- Establishing and enhancing your credibility

- Using creative techniques to enhance your business proposal

- Gathering data to include in your proposal

- Creating an outline for your proposal

In the Writing section, you will go through the process of writing your business proposal, including sections on:

- Using visuals in your business proposal

- Costing your proposal

- Writing case studies to improve your credibility

In the Presentation section, you will learn about:

- Constructing effective visuals

- Presenting your proposal to an audience

- Using body language and humor to increase the effectiveness of your presentation

- Closing the sale

This guide to successful business proposals also includes examples of different types and styles of business proposals, including:

- Sales proposals to clients

- Letters and memos as business proposals

- Proposals to government entities

- Internal proposals to top management

- Business plans as a special type of business proposal

CHAPTER 1

BUSINESS PROPOSALS 101

You may be a professional, perhaps an architect, a graphic artist, or a freelance writer. Or you may be a new salesperson at a manufacturing company or a new business owner offering products or services to a local market. Perhaps you are a contractor selling a product to a government agency. All of these professionals have something in common — they must write business proposals. If you have purchased this book, you are probably in one of these situations, and you are faced with writing your first business proposal. If you have not done this before, you may be wondering how to get started and how to put together a proposal that will successfully achieve your goal:

- To get the new client for your professional services

- To sell the product to the customer

- To get the bank loan for your business

- To get the contract

There is nothing magical about writing a business proposal, nor is it as difficult as you may think.

This book will take you through the process of writing a business proposal and will help you learn the key to success: getting your proposal accepted.

This section will review some of the common terms and concepts associated with the preparation and writing of business proposals.

What Is a Business Proposal?

A business proposal is a business document that presents information, analyzes that information, and presents a specific request to the reader. A proposal can be as short as a one-page letter or as long as hundreds of pages of detailed charts, graphs, and specifications.

Business proposals ask for decisions, usually involving commitment of resources (time, money, and people). Some proposals ask for the person to buy something, either your professional time, a product you are selling, or a service you are providing. Other business proposals ask for money for funding a project, like a business startup or growth. Still other business proposals ask for a contract to perform a service or manufacture a product over a period of time.

The important thing to remember about business proposals is that they are, explicitly and implicitly, sales and marketing documents. When you write a business proposal, your goal is a sale. You want a client to buy something from you, whether it is your time and expertise, your product, or your company's services. Even special types of proposals, like business plans, are marketing documents, because they seek someone to "buy" the company's proposition, in the form of financial support. Keeping in mind the essential nature of a business proposal helps to keep you focused on how to best structure the content and form to achieve your sales or marketing objective.

Business proposals communicate their objectives through a written document and, most often, a presentation. Both pieces of the proposal are important. A great written proposal document followed by a poor presentation has a limited chance for success; a fantastic presentation with poor documentation also will not succeed. If you are reading this book because you want to learn how to succeed at business proposals, be sure to read, understand, and incorporate both portions of the proposal (the document and the presentation) into your planning process. Learning to be an excellent proposal writer *and* presenter will magnify your chances of success a thousand fold.

Note that a proposal is not a bid or a quote. A bid is a specific document that describes price and materials, often in the context of a construction project. A bid or quote merely lists the elements of the project and provides a detailed estimate of the materials and labor needed, summarizing the project in a total price and estimated date of completion. A bid or quote does not include all of the background information about the proposing company, an executive Summary, or other key pieces of information about the project.

Format of a Business Proposal

No matter what type of business proposal you create, you will find that they all contain common elements. Some proposals have all of these elements, and some contain fewer or additional elements, but they are essentially similar. Effective business proposals have the following elements in common:

1. An executive summary, which is a separate mini-proposal providing the busy executive with the key information in the proposal.

2. An introduction, including background information on why the proposal is being written and the history of the problem or issue being addressed.

3. The body of the report, in which the topic is discussed in a logical order, with evidence presented in the form of charts, graphs, tables, and other visuals.

4. The conclusion and recommendation, which usually makes a specific request to the reader.

5. Appendixes and additional information the reader may need in order to make a decision.

6. A glossary of terms, which explains technical jargon or elucidates specialized information.

This book will discuss all of these sections of the business proposal in greater detail below.

Request for Proposal

You may have heard of a "Request for Proposal" (RFP). This document is a request by a company, nonprofit organization, or government body for suppliers or contractors to make a proposal for a specific product or service. The RFP includes details on what is needed and specifications on the project, including timeline, costs, and types of materials to be used. Clear and measurable objectives for the business proposal should be included, as well as your plan for evaluating these objectives. An RFP is a way for an organization to ask for proposals from vendors or contractors, by setting out the requirements for work or for a grant and specifying how the work is to be done or how the grant will be awarded.

For example, the military may prepare an RFP for a new electronic system on an airplane. The RFP is sent out to contractors who use the information to prepare bids on the project. In another example, a nonprofit foundation may send out a request for proposal describing a grant program to which communities may apply. The outline of the RFP in this case would likely include:

- An executive summary

- Introduction and background of the organization

- Brief problem discussion — why the RFP is being written

- How results will be measured

- Budget details

- Project timeline (preparation and time to implementation)

- Appendixes with supporting documentation, letters of support, and recommendation

- Project Description, including:

  - Goals and objectives

  - Activities to be funded

  - Length of project and key benchmarks

  - Key staff and administrators, including bios

Analyzing a Request for Proposal

If you are writing a proposal in response to an RFP, there are steps you should take to analyze the RFP before you begin writing the proposal. First, skim through the RFP to get a general sense of what the organization is asking.

Read the executive summary, looking for key words and phrases that are repeated. Read chapter and section headings. If there is an index, skim through it to see what words and phrases appear most often.

In your initial reading of the RFP, particularly note three areas of requirements:

1. Note any requirements that you feel you will not be able to meet. Later, think about whether there are ways you can meet the intent, if not the specifics, of that requirement. Just because you cannot meet all of the requirements, it does not mean your proposal will not be awarded the project. You may need to exceed expectations in one area to compensate for lack of compliance in another.

2. Note any requirements for which you feel you can exceed expectations and which may be "highlights" or areas of excellence for you and your company. As you prepare your response, you should spend more time responding in these areas, to enhance your chances of winning the job.

3. Note any areas that you feel may be "deal breakers," either in a positive or negative sense. A "deal breaker" is a key requirement on which other requirements are based. If a deal breaker requirement is one where you excel, you can move ahead with confidence in your chances of having your proposal accepted. If, on the other hand, a deal breaker is one where you have little or no chance of being able to comply, you may want to decide to pass on the opportunity. This initial review is critical to give you a clear picture of your chances, so you do not spend too much time and energy responding to an RFP that you will not be likely to win.

Here are more questions to ask yourself as you are doing an initial review of the RFP:

1. Has your company worked with this company or agency before? Does this prior relationship boost your chances of winning this proposal? If you have done work previously with this company or agency, you probably have a good chance of winning the bid. If you

have not, you will probably be at a disadvantage, since many bids go to incumbents.

2. What is the relationship of the company producing the RFP with previous vendors? If you can find out more about previous work done by other vendors, you may be able to determine if you have a good chance of taking over this work. If the company is satisfied with its current vendor, you probably have little chance, but if the relationship is poor, this may be your opportunity to step in.

3. Does the RFP seem to favor a specific vendor? If you can detect language that points to one vendor, possibly the current one, it may not be possible to override that bias.

4. Is this a serious project with appropriate funding? Find out as much as you can about the project and the company's intent before you spend time bidding. Some companies create RFPs merely to gather information, with no intent to proceed. In other cases, the company wants the project, but has little or no funding set aside to finance it.

5. Is this project profitable? What expenditures of time and money would be necessary to complete this project? Does the income from this project exceed your expenditures? Spend as much time as possible researching the details of the project so you know your costs. Although it is never possible to know exactly what it will take you to complete a project, the closer you can come to an accurate number, the better you will be able to determine if you want to bid on this project.

6. Will the project further your career or provide you with a great reference? In some cases, you may decide to bid on a project, even though it is not profitable or it will take longer than you want to spend, if there are other benefits. For example, a professional may

take on a project for little gain if it results in publicity or notice, or if it would provide an excellent reference from a key company or individual in the industry.

If you have decided it is worth your time to develop a proposal from this RFP, read through the document a second time. During this reading, take notes in the margins.

- Note areas where you have a positive advantage over competitors, and areas where you are at a disadvantage.

- Note places where you can present specific examples of your previous work to show your capabilities.

- Note any discrepancies, contradictions, or conflicts in the wording of the RFP, so you can decide later how to deal with these.

- Note areas where you will need legal assistance, for example, in a section where you may need to disclose proprietary information.

- Note areas where you will need to obtain specific financial data to use in your reply.

- Note any questions you may have about the requirements of the RFP, about terminology used, about the timeline, and about your responsibilities if your proposal is accepted.

After your initial readings of the RFP document, use the headings of the RFP to prepare a rough initial draft of your response. In other words, follow the guidelines and requirements set out in the RFP and briefly list your response to each. Many RFPs include a requirement that you respond in a specific format, and they list a series of items which must be completed in your response. If you begin by using the format requested, you will be able to stay on track and within the requirements with your response. It is important that your proposal in response to the RFP follows the specified guidelines and that you fully and completely answer every question and include every issue in the RFP.

Specifically note:

- Deadline, timeline, and all interim reporting points or due dates

- Contact names and addresses

- Required method of reply (e-mail, fax, or print, for example)

- Methods for submitting questions or clarifications

- Requirements for including subcontractors

- Invoicing requirements, payment schedules, and payment methods

- Ownership of the work product

- Legal terms and conditions

Also, note all format and reply guidelines, including limit on pages, font sizes, margins, use of color, and guidelines for use of graphics. Be careful to stay within the format guidelines for this proposal. Many proposals, especially those submitted to government agencies, have been refused because they did not adhere to specified guidelines. This may seem restrictive, but if you cannot follow directions on something as simple as a font size, a contractor will not have confidence that you will follow directions on larger issues during the project.

If you have noted questions while reading the RFP, contact the company or agency in the manner specified to ask these questions. Get your questions answered immediately after you read the RFP, so you have time to work on your proposal with complete knowledge of the requirements. Some companies or agencies will set up a bidder's conference at which all bidders can ask questions and receive answers at the same time. If a bidder's conference is part of the process for this RFP, you should plan on attending.

Here are some points to remember when reviewing and responding to an RFP:

- Perform an initial review, noting strong points and weaknesses, to make a decision about proceeding with a proposal for this project.

- Review the proposal several times to be sure you understand what is required. If you have questions, ask them early in the process so you do not waste time going in the wrong direction.

- Use profitability as your main decision point, but consider accepting an unprofitable project if you can use it to gain publicity or increase your reputation in your field.

- Respond using the format provided in the RFP. Do not deviate from this format if you want your proposal to be accepted.

- Follow all directions and requirements of the RFP, down to the smallest detail. Failure to follow directions can result in your proposal being rejected.

- Review your proposal carefully before you submit it, to make certain you have followed the format, followed directions, and complied with all requirements. Be sure to check for accuracy and for sentence errors.

- Turn the proposal in on time and in the manner required.

As a final note on this subject, if you receive an RFP, you may be able to win the customer to your proposal by developing a relationship with that company. This tactic will not work with government agencies, which are bound by strict guidelines of non-discrimination, but you may consider it for a non-governmental company. Some companies put out RFPs in the hope they will find a good company to work with, and they would be happy to dispense with the RFP if that vendor was available.

CASE STUDY: DAVID SELK

Job Captain
OPN Architects
Cedar Rapids, Iowa
319-363-6018
opn@opnarchitects.com

Our firm assembles marketing packets to respond to RFPs, and we participate in presentations with potential clients looking for architectural services. We offer architecture, interior design, and landscape architecture services.

Proposals are planned and executed by the marketing director and the principals (partners) of the firm. The number of people who attend a presentation depends on the size and complexity of the project being sought. If a project calls for all the disciplines we offer, there is a reason to have a representative from each discipline at the presentation. If a project only needs interior design services, only an interior designer will attend and a principal. There is always a principal at a presentation and the marketing director is always involved in the planning of the presentation.

The last presentation I was involved with was a fairly large, complex project, so it was decided to have a representative from each discipline of the project at the presentation, so there were six people on the presentation. We were told by the customer that we would only have 15 minutes of presentation time, with an additional 15 minutes of Q&A time. The challenge we had was to get as much meaningful information as possible conveyed to the potential client in a short time frame and allow everyone involved time to present.

We decided to use PowerPoint for the presentation, and the rough outline of the slides was put together by the marketing director. As a group, we ran through the slides and decided which ones would stay, and which ones would be deleted; we also decided on alterations that needed to be made to the slides that made the cut. Decisions were very much a group effort, but final decisions were made by the principal in charge, with the marketing director having heavy influence, and ultimately some of the final decision.

CASE STUDY: DAVID SELK

To rehearse for the presentation, we held three meetings. The first meeting we spent just going through the rough outline of slides and deciding which ones should go, which should stay, and which ones would be added. We also talked about what we should say for each slide, and the participants in the presentation were told which slides they would be responsible for.

The second meeting, we were asked to arrive prepared with the words we wanted to say for our assigned slides. We went through the slides again, and discussed as a group what was going to be said for each slide. We got much, much closer to deciding the order in which the slides would be presented. Some slides were deleted, some were added, and most of the slides were altered in some way during this meeting. The marketing director and principal decided who was going to speak for each slide. The individuals put together ideas of what they wanted to say for their individual parts but it was the marketing director who made the final decision on exactly what was to be said.

The final meeting was the day before the presentation and was an intense meeting with the same activities as the second meeting, but just more final in nature. The goal of this meeting was to work until a run-through of the presentation was completed and everyone was comfortable with what they were saying and the length of the presentation was within the time limit of 15 minutes. This meeting took about four hours and countless presentation "dry runs" until we got it right. The hardest part of this process for everyone was condensing what to say so we would be concise and our amount of time would be well-used. There was no time in this presentation for wordiness; we had to confine everything to 15 minutes.

The biggest mistakes we have made in presentations were when we were not fully prepared for the presentation. For this particular presentation, we were very prepared. Unfortunately, our proposal was not accepted for political reasons (the project was for a building in a neighboring city). We have learned that we must go over the presentation again, and again, and again. We have multiple people review the presentation before it goes to final printing. We then review the proposal document before it is sent out.

I would give this advice to others for presentations: Just be yourself. A lot of what you say is getting the client's attention. If you get the job, you will have to work with this client for a long time, and you don't want to have to keep pretending to be something you are not for that long a time.

Types of Business Proposals

Within the broad realm of business proposals, there are two different categories: the first category is internal proposals and external proposals, and the second category is solicited and unsolicited proposals.

- **Internal Proposals.** Internal proposals are produced within a business. Usually these are created by middle-level managers in larger companies and presented to top executives who want information on possible projects to be undertaken by the company. Internal proposals may be solicited or unsolicited.

- **External Proposals.** External proposals are produced by a business or a professional for a customer. These proposals may be either solicited or unsolicited.

- **Solicited Proposals.** Solicited proposals are those written and presented in response to a request by a higher-level manager or by a potential customer or client. Solicited proposals may also take the form of an RFP. An internal solicited proposal is usually written at the request of the top executives because they are interested in taking on some project. For example, the top management in a company may decide they are interested in creating a fitness center or daycare center for the use of their employees, and they ask the financial department to create such a proposal. The advantage to a solicited proposal is that it has a greater likelihood of being accepted, since the requester has already expressed interest in the project.

- **Unsolicited Proposals.** Unsolicited proposals are those presented to higher-level managers within a company or to a potential customer or client without any guarantee that the proposal will be considered, much less be accepted. Unsolicited proposals are risky, because they involve a great deal of time and effort.

While the possibilities for business proposals within these broad categories are unlimited, it is possible to separate them by type for discussion purposes. Here are the major categories of proposals to be discussed in this book:

- **Proposals by professionals.** Many professionals — from architects and artists to writers and information technology people — must write proposals for a living. Most of these individuals create a template that they use for proposals. Some re-create a new document each time, including a general description of their company and services. If you are just starting out as a professional, this book can help you set up your business proposal template, so that when an opportunity to present a proposal comes up, you will be ready to respond to it.

- **Proposals written in response to RFPs.** Some professional proposals are written in response to a request, similar to an RFP, by a client. For example, an advertising agency may present a proposal for a new advertising campaign to a client, or an architectural firm may present a proposal for a new building to a prospect. In some cases, there is competition between the various contractors or suppliers, and in other cases, you may be the only company responding, because the RFP was created solely for you. In either case, you must be prepared to respond specifically to the RFP to receive the approval for the contract.

- **Sales and marketing proposals.** Some sales and marketing proposals are presented to describe services you and your company will provide. These proposals may be presented by salespeople asking the client to buy a product or service, or they may be presentations relating to marketing or advertising a product or service. An example is a sales team that comes in to sell a company on a new computer network or integrated phone service. In other cases, a company may prepare an unsolicited advertising proposal, which is sent to a number of potential customers to determine interest in the company's services. In this case, the proposal is shorter and is written in the form of a letter or memo.

- **Proposals by businesspeople for startup and growth.** If you are in a solo business, you will need to write several business proposals, including a startup business plan or a business plan to fund the growth and development of your company. The business plan is a special form of business proposal that includes details on the company's plans for the use of funds. Business plans are essentially sales proposals, because they are written to sell a banker, lender, or venture capitalist on the viability of a business venture to secure funding. Successful businesses write business plans, not only to obtain funds, but to set a course of action and to detail the company's vision and mission. By reading this book, you will learn the details of preparing a business plan to obtain funds for startup and growth.

- **Proposals by contractors to government entities.** Companies that sell products or services to government entities must prepare proposals and bid on projects, usually in competition with other similar companies. Many business proposals are written in response to an RFP that details the needs of the government entity and the precise specifications under which each bidder must present a bid and proposal. This section will include a review of the process of responding to an RFP and preparing a proposal for a government entity, and a look at some sources of information on where to find projects and products open for bid and proposal.

Before You Begin Your Proposal

Before you begin writing a business proposal, you will need to gather information so you can be sure you are writing to the needs of the customer or client. Chapter 4 will discuss this subject in more detail. You will also need to be able to answer some specific questions:

- **Who is the client or customer?** If your proposal is to a bank, is it directed to a specific individual or department head, or is it being sent directly to a vice president? In other words, who is the decision maker? If your customer is a business, find out as much as you can about the company. If the client is an individual, the same principle applies. You need to know who you are going to be talking to before you write your proposal.

- **What is the customer or client specifically asking for?** If an RFP is involved, study it closely. Ask yourself what the customer wants. You should be able to state the client's request in one sentence, with as much detail as possible. For example, "The client wants a new contemporary-looking public library built." Or, "The customer wants a copier/printer/fax system throughout the office, with at least 12 stations in the system."

- **Who will evaluate the proposal?** Know the players and their personalities. If there is a committee involved, you need to spend time with the members so you get to know their individual likes and dislikes. Try to determine who will be the primary decision maker and pay particular attention to that person. If the client is an individual person or a small business owner, determine what he or she needs. Often, the client's stated need and his or her real need are not the same. The only way to gain an understanding of clients is to spend time with them. If you are not able to do this in person, you may have to settle for a few phone conversations.

- **Are there multiple levels of decision makers involved?** In business plan proposals to banks, for example, the local loan officer may send your proposal to a loan committee. Asking about levels helps you determine the importance of an executive summary and how to write this portion of the proposal.

- **Can you win before the proposal is written?** In some proposal situations, it is ethical for you to get information from the client about priorities, personal preferences, or political traps to avoid. This information is extremely valuable, because it allows you to tailor the proposal to the client's needs.

- **Have you lost before the proposal is submitted?** In some situations, your proposal is requested to compare it to another, preferred proposal. This means that your chances of getting the sale or the work are not good. Of course, you should always do your utmost to get the work, but this knowledge can help you determine what resources to commit to the proposal.

Keys to Creating Successful Business Proposals

As you plan the business proposal you are writing, you may wonder what you should do to ensure that your proposal will be successful. While many elements need to be considered, there are several key elements that experts say will make or break your proposal. As you begin writing, think about how these four keys can assist you in creating an award-winning business proposal:

Key 1: Writing Style. Write in a clear, direct style with correct spelling and grammar. Many proposals are poorly written; these proposals are not read. If you do not take the time to write clearly and correctly, your prospective client will not take the time to seriously consider your proposal. See Chapter 7 for a discussion of the "7 Cs" of business proposal writing.

Key 2: Objective. Take time to formulate a clear objective for your proposal. Ask yourself what you want the reader to do with the information that you are providing. Having a clear objective allows you to gear the proposal toward supporting and explaining that objective and it will help your reader understand what you want. Chapter 4 will take you through the process of constructing a clear objective for your business proposal, and examine how to stay on track with that objective throughout the document.

Key 3: Completeness. To ensure a successful proposal, you must be certain that you leave no question in the reader's mind. If your reader has a question or a concern that you do not address, the reader will continue to think about that concern and will not focus on your proposal or your presentation of that proposal. An unaddressed question can stop a proposal from being accepted. For example, if you are giving a proposal about a new business you want to start and you fail to address the question of competition, your reader will think you do not understand the importance of competition and may wonder whether you realize you have competitors and understand how it can impact your business. Instead of listening to you talk about the great positive points of your proposal, your reader or listener is thinking about the negative point you failed to address.

Key 4: Use the KISS Principle. The KISS principle is: Keep it Short and Simple. While you must be complete in your writing, you should include only the essential information. Adding extraneous and wordy explanations, or providing technical language and jargon will not only confuse your reader, but it can cause the client to dismiss your proposal. Only include the information that is required in your business proposal, and use clear, concise language. In chapter 4 of this book, the elements of this key concept is covered in more detail.

Following Directions in Proposal Writing

There is one more key element to address regarding the writing of business proposals: Follow directions. Although it seems very obvious, it is at the core of every business proposal. Proposals that succeed follow the directions imposed by the client or customer. Proposals that fail probably did not follow the directions.

If you are responding to an RFP, for example, it is important that you completely answer all of the questions addressed by the client. If the client is the United States government, not following directions is a reason for your proposal to be discarded. If the client requests a list of references of previous clients, provide them. If the client wants you to discuss your timeline, include it.

Do not include information your client has specifically requested you not to include. If the client has requested that you not include examples of work from previous clients, do not include them. If you are not sure whether to include something, do not hesitate to ask. Clients will appreciate your willingness to adhere to their requirements.

Writers and graphic artists often respond to advertisements for positions. These ads include specific requirements for work samples, references from previous clients, and citations or a bibliography. Failure to address these requirements can result in the proposal being returned. Something as simple as the preferred form of correspondence — a SASE (self-addressed stamped envelope) or e-mail — can cause the proposal to be rejected.

Should You Write the Proposal?

Before you begin to spend the time and money to prepare a proposal, you should consider some circumstances under which it makes no sense for you to write a proposal. Here are some factors to consider when deciding whether or not to write a proposal:

1. **What is the maximum amount you can make on this project?** Sometimes, the budget for a project is so small it is not worth your time and money to prepare and present a proposal. If the client has indicated, for example, that he or she will not pay more than $1000 for the project, you should spend time calculating your cost for this project, including your time and energy in preparing the proposal. If your cost exceeds the expected return, you should not begin work on this proposal. In some freelance professions, like graphic arts and freelance writing, figuring the time it will take you to complete the assignment against your desired or required hourly rate may reveal you are working for a very low hourly rate. Consider the value of your time and the other projects you can take on during this time. Including these factors in the equation may lead you to turn down the opportunity to write a proposal.

2. **Who is your competition?** If there are a number of other companies writing proposals in competition with you, you may feel your chances of receiving the project are low. In particular, if one of the competitors is already doing work for the client, they may have the edge. On the other hand, some companies routinely put projects up for proposal to force a current vendor to lower his or her price, or to find another vendor who will work more cheaply. Depending on your ability to come in with a lower-cost proposal, you may have an advantage in this competitive situation. A careful evaluation of the pool of competitors and the competitive situation can help you determine whether or not to prepare a proposal in a specific situation.

3. **Do you have enough information to write the proposal?** If the company has put out an RFP, review the document carefully. Verify that the RFP is carefully laid out and completely explains what the

company wants. A vague, poorly written, or incomplete RFP may be a sign that the company does not know what it wants or does not know how to state what it wants. In this case, preparing a proposal may be an exercise in futility. If the client is not clear in describing what he or she wants, how do you know you can fulfill the request? Lack of a clear RFP may be a sign there is conflict among the top administrators, or the individual is confused about the project. You may save yourself a lot of frustration by walking away from poorly thought out requests.

4. **What are the long-term implications of presenting this proposal?** If you are in the business of writing proposals and fulfilling their terms, you are building a professional expertise in a specific area. Each proposal has the potential to add to your credentials. Some proposals may not add much to your resumé, but they may provide you with an entrance to a company you want to work with and a provider-client relationship you want to pursue. Before you prepare a proposal on a project, you should carefully evaluate whether this project will enhance your professional reputation or will bring you into contact with people you feel are essential to your success. If the project does neither, you should consider not taking it. The opportunity cost of working on a dead-end proposal while having to pass up a proposal with long-term benefits is too high. Save your energy and work on securing better projects.

5. **Is the timing right for this proposal?** Sometimes, a great proposal opportunity comes along at the wrong time. If taking on a particular project means you will have to sacrifice quality to do the work, you may be better off saying no. If you are overcommitted, you may find you do not do justice to your current work or to this new proposal, sacrificing family and health in the process.

Determining whether or not to take on a proposal and project means carefully assessing the situation, considering the costs of taking on the project, and weighing the alternatives. Although it is often a difficult decision to make, sometimes the best choice, for one or more reasons, is to say no to a proposal and project.

If you decide not to submit a proposal, you need to decline gracefully and carefully. Here are some tips to consider when saying no to a business project:

- **Consider the relationship.** Your primary concern in saying no should be the preservation of the relationship between your company and the client. If you have submitted other proposals to this client before, your refusal may be taken personally. Spend time thinking about the words you will use and the reasons you will put forth to the client. If you have not previously done work for this client, you should still be careful to present the "no" in as positive a light as possible, so you have the opportunity to make proposals in the future.

- **Say no in person.** You want to be able to answer questions and to assure the client there are no hard feelings. If an in-person discussion is not possible, the next best alternative is over the phone. Only if a personal visit or phone call is not possible should you say no through mail or e-mail.

- **Be courteous and professional.** What "goes without saying" sometimes needs to be said, so make sure your language is courteous and puts your client at ease. Take the time to chat with the client about the proposal. Avoid personal comments about the client or the client's company.

The Agreement Letter:
An Alternative to the Proposal

In some cases, it might not be worthwhile to prepare a full proposal for a client. Unfortunately, many individuals and companies request proposals to fill other needs, when they have no intention of accepting the proposal.

CASE STUDY: JOHN COYNE

Pivot Business Resources, LLC
13331 E. Del Timbre Drive
Scottsdale, AZ 85259
480-657-7757
info@pivotu.com

John Coyne, of Pivot Business Resources, LLC, has been presenting business proposals for many years. Over this time, he has been involved in many sales presentations where a prospective client requested a proposal and the vendor thinks the sale is imminent.

If you are in that position, you may be tempted to spend time writing and refining the proposal, only to be told when you present it that the client is not really interested. There are several reasons why the person may want your proposal including:

1.   He or she is price shopping, trying to find the vendor with the lowest priced product.

2.   He or she is attempting to delay or derail the sales process and has no intention of going through with the sale.

In these circumstances, John suggests you avoid presenting a sales proposal and instead close the sale verbally and prepare a letter of agreement. The agreement letter would contain all of the elements of the proposal, but it would be presented to the client as a fait accompli (a "done deal"), requiring only the client's signature for the sale to be accomplished.

Closing a client on an agreement is the key to this process. You must first determine if the prospective client is a serious customer or a "tire kicker." Some clues may

CASE STUDY: JOHN COYNE

be the client's expressed sense of urgency about the timing, and the specifics of the discussion. In the case where you suspect a prospect is price shopping or not committed to the sale, try to get him or her to discuss specifics, timelines, and, most important, general pricing. If the client balks, you may suspect you are dealing with a "tire kicker."

John suggests that in these cases you attempt to move the client toward an agreement letter, rather than a proposal. State that you would be happy to put together a proposal. Before you write up the proposal, state that you need to be assured the client is in a position to make a decision. Let the person know you expect an answer immediately upon presentation of the agreement letter. If you have this pre-agreement discussion and the person does not commit to an answer, you have not wasted your time putting together a lengthy and costly proposal only to have it rejected.

John Coyne

Pivot Business Resources has a primary mission of helping client companies achieve dramatically improved results in four key areas:

- Improved financial performance

- Enhanced ability to lead and manage

- Strengthened relationships with customers

- Renewed growth and innovation

Pivot works with companies to assess performance across key business discipline areas and, where appropriate, build action plans for improvement.

Why Some Proposals Do Not Succeed and What to Do About It

If you prepared a business proposal that did not succeed, you may have decided to read this book to find out how to do a better job at writing a proposal. Or you may have talked to someone in your company or in another company who complained that a proposal was not accepted. If you are wondering why some business proposals do not succeed, here are some suggestions to help you avoid the problems that keep business proposals from succeeding.

It is possible that a proposal did not succeed for a straightforward reason, like another proposal had a lower cost. But many times, the failure is in the content of the proposal itself. For example:

- The proposal was a "data dump," in which the writer simply included language from previous proposals, or from product or sales literature, adding descriptive language about the client and about his or her own company, with little thought to the issues or problems of the client.

- The proposal lacked planning, with no thought about how to present the material in a logical and organized fashion, leading to a disorganized mess.

- The proposal did not include relevant graphs, tables, or figures, or, worse, it may have included irrelevant or useless graphics.

- The proposal did not address the needs of the client, or not take into account the various levels of decision makers within the client's organization.

- The proposal did not include an executive summary to help the client executives and decision makers see the big picture.

- The proposal contained confusing language, technical jargon, and complex explanations of processes and procedures.

- The proposal was not detailed enough, offering only superficial or trivial solutions to the client's problems.

- The proposal writer did not take the time to create a comprehensive proposal. He or she may have used a company brochure with a cover letter and a price quote or catalog.

- The proposal was not interesting to read.

- The proposal lacked focus, trying to be everything to everyone and pleasing no one.

- The proposal was too self-centered, focusing only on the presenting organization and not on the client's needs and proposal requirements.

- The proposal did not include a "call to action" to ask for the sale.

One major reason many proposals do not succeed is their reliance on "boilerplate" language. The term "boilerplate" comes from the steel sheets used in manufacturing boilers. The printing industry in the late 19th and 20th centuries used similar steel sheets for printing pages of newspapers and other mass-produced documents. In this way, boilerplate began to stand for a document that was mass produced and not individually printed. In the legal profession, boilerplate (or "standard") phrases have come to be a part of many contracts.

There are parts of a business proposal where you may want to include boilerplate information. For example, you may want to include a prepared paragraph or two about your company and your company history, because these paragraphs have been previously approved by your company, or you may want to include brief biographies of the people responsible for the preparation of the proposal and for administration of the project or services. In this case, briefly review the language to make certain there is nothing that may cause a problem or detract from your presentation.

In another example of boilerplate, you may want to include a brief description of the client, to show that you know the client's background; this information may be taken from an annual report or other document, or from a description of the client's company from a Web site. On the other hand, you may want to spend more time and prepare your own paragraphs about the client and his or her company, to better emphasize the time and attention you have given to understanding this client.

If you have product specifications from sales brochures and manuals, you may want to include these verbatim to prevent inadvertent errors. Keep these descriptions to a minimum, though, to avoid the appearance of too much boilerplate.

The best rule of thumb regarding boilerplate is to avoid it as much as possible. You can use general language from previous proposals, but take the time to make modifications and alterations to suit the needs of the client and the specific proposal you are writing.

In the rest of this business proposal guide, you will find many strategies to help you avoid the problems outlined above.

- Chapter 4 provides a process for planning your business proposal so that it is easy to read and provides an organized structure for your client to follow.

- Chapter 5 includes a discussion on meeting client's technical, financial, and personal needs.

- Chapter 7 provides guidelines on writing style, avoiding sentence errors, and keeping your business proposal short and to the point.

- Chapter 10 includes information on avoiding "data dump" and boilerplate language, and for preparing a proposal specifically relevant to the client's specific needs.

- Chapter 15 discusses the concept of the executive summary, its importance, and how to write this portion of your business proposal.

- Chapter 18 discusses the use of visuals for the proposal and the presentation, and how to make these visuals interesting, easy to read, and relevant to your client.

CHAPTER 2

ETHICAL CONSIDERATIONS: WHAT NOT TO WRITE

This chapter will discuss ethical considerations involved in writing business proposals. There are many pitfalls in this subject, and this chapter will focus on some of the more treacherous ones.

Creating False Impressions

Business proposals should be as factual as possible. Of course, there is a certain amount of personal bias in anything, even a business document, but you will need to be careful to keep your tone and wording as objective as possible, and not to slant your language or present information in a false light. Here is some advice on two potentially sensitive topics:

- **Competition.** If you are considering including negative information about your competitors, be sure you are factual. In most cases, it is best to leave out this information. If you include it, you are taking a chance that the client may be turned off and reject your proposal.

- **Testimonials.** Presenting opinions about your product or service is certainly acceptable; testimonials are always a good sales device. Make sure the testimonials are from real people and are complete. The best testimonials are unsolicited, spontaneous, and in writing.

- **Keep it positive.** Avoid language that may be slanted against others. It is acceptable to talk about your own products or services, but it is not professional to be negative about the products or services of your competitors. For example, if you are selling copiers, you can talk about the benefits of your company's copiers, and compare features and benefits of your copiers with those of your competitors in a table. If you go too far and discuss things that are wrong with your competitors' copiers, you may be sued for libel by that company.

Making statements that can damage the reputation of an individual or company falls under the general title of "defamation of character," and the person or company being defamed has the right to bring a lawsuit against you to stop you from continuing this behavior. You may have to pay large amounts of money in punitive damages (for punishment). Think carefully about how to approach comparisons of your products or services with those of others. Your best approach is to avoid such comparisons and to concentrate on your own great products or services.

Incomplete, Misleading, or Inaccurate Information

When preparing your proposal, be sure to provide as much information about your product or service as possible. If there is research, for example, that shows your product has a problem, it is best to discuss it. You may be able to minimize the damage by showing the research is false or incomplete.

Ignoring an issue only raises questions. This subject is important because it can be the downfall of your entire proposal if not handled right. Let us say you are presenting a proposal to a company about your copiers, and you leave out a vital piece of research that shows your copiers have been known to cause injury to people. It is almost inevitable that someone at the company has read the report on the Internet, and you will be challenged about this issue.

Leaving out or falsifying important information about your products or services may cause you to be sued by the client for fraud. Fraud, in its broadest sense, is deceiving someone for personal gain.

Consider alternate points of view for completeness. If you can prepare alternative suggestions for the proposal, you may interest people on the review committee who may not have liked the original proposal.

Sexist, Racist, or Demeaning Language

Being intentionally offensive to others is never appropriate, but even unintentional sexist or biased language has no place in a business proposal. Using sexual, racial, or religious references may turn your reader off about the entire report and can cost you the contract or the work. One word can make the difference. For example, the use of a sexist term like "girl" to refer to an administrative assistant can mean the difference between getting your proposal accepted or not. Here are some examples of biased language, which need to be avoided:

- The stewardess gave the usual preflight speech to the passengers. Use: "flight attendant."

- The African-American vice president of public relations was the first speaker last night. Use: "The vice president of public relations was the first speaker last night."

- Slang terms that apply to certain groups, such as "to gyp" someone or "Jew someone down," are not acceptable. The easiest way to avoid this kind of reference is to avoid using slang in any form. Slang has no place in a professional business proposal.

The "he or she" problem. All nonfiction writers face this issue. Some writers attempt to avoid it altogether, but that is almost impossible. If you are talking about a process, for example, it is difficult to imagine how you will finish this sentence without having problems: "Each employee was asked to complete (his? his or her?) benefits election before the end of the month."

To avoid this issue, here are some suggestions:

- Use the plural, as in: "All employees were asked to complete their benefits election forms before the end of the month."

- Break a grammatical rule and make a singular pronoun agree with a plural one. "Each employee was asked to complete their benefits election form before the end of the month."

- Use his/her. This is neither grammatically correct nor pleasing in sound.

- Alternate the use of "his" and "her." In a long document, this works well, but it may be confusing in a short document.

- State at the beginning of the work that you are using the masculine as a generic pronoun to represent both the male and female. In this case, you are assuming your reader has read the note at the beginning.

None of these solutions is perfectly acceptable. Using "his or her" is probably the best and least confusing solution. This book alternates between the male and female pronoun, so that as the reader goes through the document, she can get a sense of balance between male and female business proposal writers.

Privacy Considerations

As you write your business proposal, you may want to include material from experts or interviews. Before including such material, you must do two things:

1. Obtain a written release asking the experts or interviewees to allow you to use their expert opinion or quotes from their interview in your proposal. The release does not need to be lengthy; it can state simply that the person gives you the approval to use the material in your proposal.

2. After you write the material, allow the expert or interviewee the opportunity to review the material before publication. If the person finds something objectionable or incorrect, be sure to change it before you complete the proposal.

Ownership and Plagiarism Issues

Another critical ownership issue is the importance of giving credit to sources you use in the proposal. For example, if you include a chart prepared by the United States Census Bureau, you must show the reader the source of this chart. Plagiarism is taking the work of others for your own use; in other words, it is theft of intellectual property. If you plagiarize, you can be sued by the person whose work you have stolen.

Plagiarism includes, but is not limited to:

1. Taking material produced by others and stating explicitly it is your own material, or implying the work is yours by not citing the work specifically in your proposal.

2. Working together with another individual and using material produced by that person without giving credit.

3. Using more than five exact words in specific order from another person's work without citing that work.

The concept of plagiarism began with the journalism and education fields. In response to the proliferation of sources available in the past 15 years through the Internet and online media, concerns about plagiarism have spread to all other fields of work. Because information on the Internet is considered "free," many people believe all information on Web sites is available without regard for citing sources. This is not true; most Web authors have copyright statements on their Web sites, and you cannot use these sites without giving credit to the authors.

What to Cite

Here is a brief list of the types of information sources to which you need to give credit:

- Words or ideas from books, newspapers, magazines, TV and radio programs, recorded media (such as CDs, DVDs, and videocassettes), advertisements, computer programs, and Internet and online sources.

- Information you learn from individuals through interviews, case studies, and conversations, on the phone and in writing. For example, all of the interviewees for this book signed permission forms stating they would allow the publisher to reprint the interviews or written statements collected for the book. In several cases, the interviewees included copyright statements.

- Reprints of visual media, including diagrams, charts, pictures, and illustrations, including those found on Web sites. Photos and other visuals included in this book taken from Internet or other sources have been cited.

The general rule of thumb for citing sources is:

- All direct quotes of five or more words in sequence must be in quotations and the source must be identified in a citation. For example, if I cite from a book about business writing and include the phrase "citations are best used sparingly," I would need to cite the source, since I included five words in sequence.

- The source of all paraphrases must be cited. For example, if I were writing about business proposals and included information from a text on writing style, even though I paraphrased (rewrote the information in my own words), I would be required to cite the source.

When You Do Not Need to Cite

To further clarify, here are some instances in which you do not need to receive permission or cite sources:

- If you write in your own words from your own experience and observations, and if you form your own conclusions or express your own opinion about a subject.

- If you create your own visuals (as I did in most cases in this book).

- If you are using an encyclopedia, dictionary, or other tertiary source, either in print or online. A tertiary source collects or summarizes information from primary or secondary sources. Tertiary sources are not the most useful for business purposes.

- If you are expressing "common knowledge" about a fact or subject. Historic events and basic biographical information about famous historical figures are common knowledge. If you can find the same information in a number of sources, it is generally considered to be "common knowledge." For example, the statement in Chapter 19 that "public speaking ranks higher than fear of death" could be considered to be common knowledge, since the reference can be found in many places, and it is difficult to determine where it originated.

A Special Case: Including Visuals in Your Proposal

If you want to include visuals (photos and illustrations), in your business proposal, there are several ways to do this:

- Create your own visuals or pay someone to create them. For example, you may want to include some photos of your company buildings; if you have paid someone to take these photos, they are your property and you do not need permission or citation for them.

- Use free sources of photos or illustrations. There are a number of online sources for free photos, including **www.morguefile.com**. These sources arrange photos by category. The quality and quantity of these photos is variable, but you may find some photos that you can use from these sources.

- Pay money for photos from an online source, like Getty Images (**www. gettyimages.com**). These sources charge for downloading and using their images, depending upon the popularity and uniqueness of the images. If you cannot find an image you are looking for, try one of these sites.

- Clip art (free drawings) may also be available at such sites as **www. freestockphotos.com** and **www.istockphoto.com**.

Avoiding Plagiarism

To avoid being charged with plagiarism in your business proposals:

- If you find information you want to use in your business proposal, write it exactly as it was written elsewhere, and put it in quotations. This will prevent you from confusing a quoted statement from a paraphrase and possibly re-quoting the source directly in your attempt to paraphrase. In other words, if you note the exact quote, you can later decide whether to keep the quote or paraphrase.

- Use your own ideas and concepts as much as possible. If there is a possibility that your ideas may be the same as those of others, you may want to check on the Internet to see if they have been stated previously in other works. One way to do this is to search for a string of words, like "public speaking fear" or "fear of public speaking" to see if these words can be found elsewhere.

- Include citations for government sources, even though they may be considered "common knowledge." Even if you would not necessarily be considered to have plagiarized this information, it is a good idea to let your reader know where you found the information.

- Cite sources for all information you find on the Internet, including visuals, documents, online videos, and other media. Include the URL of the Web site where you found the information.

In conclusion, when in doubt, cite your sources. Cite all quotations of five or more words, and cite sources for words and phrases you have paraphrased.

CHAPTER 3

KEY ELEMENTS
IN SUCCESSFUL PROPOSALS

Solutions

A successful proposal provides a specific solution to a specific problem. For example:

- A company needs a new advertising campaign to market a new line of products. The advertising agency creates a proposal showing the company how it can effectively market these products.

- A dentist may have the problem of growing quickly and needing to expand into an adjoining space in a strip mall. In this case, the company will prepare a proposal to take to a bank to obtain the additional funding.

- The United States Army may have the problem of finding a new contractor to produce trucks for use in the hilly, rough terrain of Afghanistan. The Army writes an RFP, and contractors respond with proposals to build these trucks.

Benefits

A successful proposal provides specific benefits to solve a specific problem set forth by a company or individual client. The benefit may be tangible, such as increased revenue; or intangible, such as increased visibility in the market or increased customer goodwill.

Credibility

A successful proposal enhances the credibility of the presenter. You will learn how to improve your credibility through knowledge of the subject, collecting expert opinions, researching the topic, and presenting your credentials.

Samples

A successful proposal includes samples of how the proposal will work, and examples of parties who have been successful using the solutions in your proposal. One sample may be a case study describing how the bidder worked with a similar company in a similar situation to solve that company's problem. Samples of previous successful solutions to problems can help you secure the acceptance of your proposal.

Target

A successful proposal is targeted carefully to appeal to a specific audience. The presenter exhibits an understanding of the needs of the target audience and knows how to use language to increase interest and obtain action. The presenter also is aware of the various audiences who will review the proposal and the specific audience who will make the decision,. The proposal is targeted to all the needs and questions of all audiences. In this book, you will see how to write effectively to a variety of audiences for your proposal.

CHAPTER 4

FOCUS ON YOUR AUDIENCE

If there is one critical factor in the success of a business proposal, it is writing to please your audience. It sounds simple, but it is a complex process of understanding the viewpoint and needs of your audience and preparing a proposal to address those needs. This section will consider all the aspects of this subject, from figuring out the specific objectives of your proposal, to considering the different types of audiences for business proposals, to writing to overcome the varying degrees of resistance of different audiences to your proposal.

First, look at some examples of poor habits in business proposal writing that show a lack of understanding of the concept of audience focus:

- A proposal by an office supply company that used copies of product brochures, rather than providing original documents.

- A proposal by a consulting company that was plainly boilerplate and provided "personalization" by inserting the client company name at relevant places in the document.

- A proposal by an office design company in which the company history of the client stopped before the current company president took office.

- A proposal by an accounting firm to a new public company that was written in highly technical language and included many terms not familiar to the new executives in the client company.

At the most basic level, these proposals fail to address the client's need to be recognized as an individual. If you are going to take the time and trouble to present a business proposal to a client, it is important that you take the time to:

- Research the most recent information about the client, the client's employees, and top executives.

- Provide original documents produced specifically for the client.

- Understand the background and technical knowledge of the client.

As you read through this section, consider the specific types of clients to whom you will be presenting business proposals, and think about how you can adapt the information provided here to your clients and the proposals you are writing.

CASE STUDY: PROPOSAL PRESENTATIONS:

A proposal manager at a company serving the higher education market works with others to provide proposals to colleges and universities for administrative software and implementation and strategic consulting services, including student, financial aid, human resources, finance, alumni, portal, workflow and other administrative products.

CLASSIFIED CASE STUDIES™
directly from the experts

The process of presenting a proposal includes:

- An account executive identifies client needs and determines whether the company's products and services can fill those needs.

- The products and services requested are identified.

CASE STUDY: PROPOSAL PRESENTATIONS:

- A strategic meeting is scheduled with the proposal response team (subject matter experts and management).

- An agenda is prepared for discussion at the meeting, highlighting all possible issues and questions.

- A workable project calendar is prepared, based on the project deadline.

- A work plan is prepared for the tasks, due dates, and participants.

The steps in planning a proposal include:

- The contents of the RFP are reviewed for a match to the products and services.

- The issues that would impede the response process are identified.

- The project calendar is built.

- The resources needed to respond to non-boilerplate requirements are identified.

- The outline of the response is developed based on the RFP requirements.

Before presentation, the document goes through multiple reviews by subject matter experts and individuals required to sign off on the presentation.

To plan the proposal presentation:

- The proposal manager works with the sales team to understand the company's sales strategy.

- They use a pre-developed proposal template with descriptions of products and services, terms and conditions, and other related materials.

- They work with sales and subject matter experts to understand the business requirements and to prepare customized responses where required.

The proposal presentation mirrors the format requirements of the RFP. The presentation is in Word format and uses graphics, picture, and text. It is provided in printed copy in a customized binder. Sometimes a CD or electronic e-mail version is included at the client's request.

CASE STUDY: PROPOSAL PRESENTATIONS:

Communication between various departments is necessary to prepare a top-quality proposal. Sales must provide a clear picture of the business strategy; the strategy cannot change in midstream, and the response team must fully understand the strategy.

The most effective proposals are those where sales has developed a relationship with the client. It is essential to present a personalized proposal to address the client's vision and objective by providing clear and direct benefit statements of the company's value, understanding the projects goals and objectives. The proposal must show the client that their requests have been listened to. Avoiding boilerplate in key sales areas of the proposal is important to keep the proposal personal and increase its effectiveness.

Some advice from this experienced project manager:

- Qualify the account. If you are not the lead vendor, it is highly unlikely that you will win the business. Do not waste time and resources on no-chance proposals.

- Understand client needs, objectives, and visions.

- Plan and coordinate your response prior to the release of the RFP. Work with sales support and other subject matter experts in supporting the process.

- Obtain buy-in from all participants before the release of the proposal.

Determining Your Objectives

First, consider your primary objective. What is the most important thing you want your client or customer to do? You may say it is "accept the proposal," but this statement is not a clear and specific objective. The more detailed and specific you are in stating your objective, the better you will be able to focus on that objective throughout the proposal.

Decide on several key objectives relating to:

- **Your client.** What are your main objectives relating to the client? Do you want to establish a long-term relationship with this client, or are you looking primarily for a one-time project? What are your objectives with regard to obtaining a recommendation or testimonial from this client?

- **Your project.** What is your main objective relating to the project? Is this a new type of project for your company, or is it a type of project with which you have had much experience? Will this project be something you can use as a basis for other projects? Will you be expanding an existing product or service to take on this project?

- **Your firm.** What is your main objective relating to your firm? Is this project intended to bring you a maximum amount of money? Will you be using the project to gain more experience in a new area? Will your firm be in a position to use this project to garner additional new work?

After you have considered your primary objectives, you will need to prioritize them to determine which ones are most important. For example, you may decide that maximizing your profit is most important in this proposal, or you may feel that beginning a good long-term relationship with the customer is most important. You can see that establishing your priorities will help you make decisions about the project and its presentation as you move into the price negotiation process (explained in Chapter 12).

Considering Types of Audiences

One of the most vital and important considerations for your business proposal is reaching your audience. To reach your audience, you must spend the time to get to know them as much as possible. If you are making a business proposal to an individual, it is easy to get to know this person and find out as much as possible about how he thinks or what her primary motive is.

In many cases, a business proposal is presented to a company in which there are several audiences, each with different needs and interests in the proposal. Here are some of the possible audiences in a company:

- **The top executive, who is the final decision maker.** This person is busy and she wants only the facts to determine whether you are the best person or company to solve her problem. In many cases, the top executive is relying on other people in the company to advise her and provide input, but remember, the top executive is the person making the final decision.

- **The vice presidents and high-level managers.** Like the top executive, these people are busy and may be relying on their subordinates to help them evaluate your proposal. They are also going to be careful to make the decision they think the top executive will be happy with, and which will be the most cost-effective solution.

- **The middle managers and technical people.** These people will be working with you to implement the proposal or to use or sell your products. They are the people you will have the most interaction with on a regular basis after your product or service proposal is accepted. You need to be sure their questions are answered completely and they are in agreement that your proposal is the best solution for the problem. If you cannot convince this level of employee of your proposal, they will not recommend it to higher-level executives.

While these interrelationships within a company are complex, you must take the time to understand them and to deal with the "politics" of the organization if you want your proposal to be successful. Here are some suggestions for dealing with these audiences:

- Prepare a clear and complete executive summary so the top executive and the vice presidents can quickly get a sense of the benefits of your proposal. This may be the only part of your proposal they see.

- Spend time discussing the technical aspects of your proposal with the middle- and lower-level people at the company. Include appendixes for these individuals, showing all of the technical detail.

- Spend time discussing the benefits of your proposal in solving the company's problem with vice presidents and those who report to the top executive. If they understand the benefits, they can portray them to the executive. Put these benefits in bullet points in the executive summary or in the body of the proposal, so they can be found easily.

Understanding Different Levels of Client Interest and Understanding

The more technical your subject, the more important it is to determine your client's level of understanding and knowledge before you present your proposal to that person.

One way to be sure you are not overreaching your audience is to write as if your readers were a level below where they actually are. People feel uncomfortable if they are forced to stretch their understanding in a situation like a business proposal, so writing down a little makes them feel more comfortable that they can handle the concepts. Do not worry that you will offend by taking this approach. The average person today reads at a fifth-grade level, and you would be surprised at how many business people read at this level. Understanding your audience gives you an advantage in preparing your written and verbal business proposal.

Here are the three different levels of readers, based on their understanding and experience with the subject of your business proposal:

The Uninformed Reader. For readers who have little or no understanding or background, you will need to give them the maximum of detail and explanation. Do not use jargon (technical words used in a profession); find simple words and phrases to explain your concepts. Do not use acronyms (shortened expressions or abbreviations); spell out all of the phrases and expressions you use in the proposal, and use as few of these expressions as possible. If you must use specialized terms, define them. Avoid obscure references to sources not readily known to the general public. For example, if you are making a proposal about a medical subject, avoid references to specialized medical journals. Lead your reader step by step through the proposal, and make sure any processes or procedures are clearly spelled out and described.

When you prepare the presentation for your proposal, keep your PowerPoint slides simple and follow the presentation principles discussed in Chapter 20. Use simple and clear charts, graphs, and tables, and make sure they are labeled to avoid misunderstanding. For this audience, adhering to the principles of the "7 Cs" (discussed in Chapter 7) is important; write in clear, short, simple, direct words and phrases.

The Informed Reader. For readers who have a general knowledge of the subject, spend time putting your proposal in context; give your reader a way to understand how this proposal fits into the bigger picture, and how you can help the reader achieve his goals through your proposal. You can use some jargon and technical terms, but only if you are certain your reader is familiar with these terms. You can also use more detailed charts, graphs, and tables, but use them sparingly and be careful not to make them too complex.

Spend time linking the new with the familiar by the use of analogies (comparisons), and while you can be more sophisticated in your use of sources and references than with the uninformed reader, always be careful not to overwhelm. Be sure your meaning is clear and that you remain centered on meeting the needs of your audience.

The Expert Reader. This reader has a detailed knowledge of and background in the technical aspects of your proposal. This person will want to know why you are making this proposal and what alternatives may be available. The expert reader will want to know how to "tweak" the process or procedure to make it work better. In a proposal for new computer software, for example, the technical person will want to know the source code and how to adjust the software for the specific user. Be prepared to spend time with this person or group in providing them with these details.

With the expert reader, you can use more jargon and technical terms if you are certain these are familiar terms to this company or individual. In many cases, you will need to provide more technical detail and background in an appendix, rather than in the body of the proposal.

Writing Proposals for Audiences at Different Levels

What if your audience includes readers and decision makers at different levels? If you are writing a business proposal for a medium-sized to large company, you may have to make a presentation to an audience which includes individuals at different levels of the organization, including technical types, top executives, and middle managers. In this case, determining one level of understanding and familiarity with your subject is difficult. Here are some tips to help you with this difficult task:

1. Use the "level down" approach. Determine the level of most of your audience, and write one level down. In other words, if most of your audience is at the "informed reader" level, you are safe in assuming they will understand simple terms and explanations.

2. Write to the top executives, who will be the ultimate decision makers. They will be at the "informed reader" level, with some understanding of and background in your subject area, but without the technical knowledge and depth of understanding. By writing to this level, in the middle, you will make them feel comfortable about their understanding of your proposal.

3. Include technical details and more advanced charts and graphs in appendixes, and talk with the technical people in a separate discussion. The executives will get bored and lose interest if you include too much technical detail, but they may allow you to spend time answering technical questions later, after your main presentation.

Considering Different Personalities of Audiences

If you want to master the art of creating successful business proposals, you need to spend time learning more about personality styles, so you can tailor your reports to these personalities. While there are many ways to categorize personality styles, there are several basic personality measures you can use. The trick is to practice recognizing the various personality styles so you can easily determine the personality style of the person for whom you are making your proposal.

There are many ways to view personality types and social interaction styles. This section is an overview of one way to understand the varied personality types of your audiences. It is based on an instrument called the Meyers-Briggs Type Indicator (MBTI). The assumptions behind this instrument are based on the work of 20th-century psychologist Carl Jung, who described the ways people use perception and judgment in combination with other attitudes. The mother-daughter team of Katharine Briggs and Isabel Briggs-Myers further developed Jung's ideas to construct an instrument which would make Jung's work accessible and useful for people who were interested in understanding themselves and others.

The MBTI instrument looks at four dichotomies of personality type to construct a picture of an individual's preferences. It does not consider traits, but rather forces a choice between four sets of alternatives to provide an overall picture of the individual type, as expressed in a four-character designation.

The four dichotomies of the MBTI are as follows:

Extroversion and Introversion (E/I) describe attitudes or orientations of energy. An individual who is high in extroversion directs her energy toward the world of people and draws energy from being with people. An individual who is high in introversion directs his energy toward the world of ideas and draws energy from his inner world.

Sensing and Intuition (S/N) describe functions or processes or perception. An individual who is high in sensing focuses on what may be perceived by the five senses. An individual who is high in intuition focuses on perceiving patterns and interrelationships between things and people.

Thinking and Feeling (T/N) describe functions or processes of judgment. An individual who is high in thinking bases her conclusions on logical argument or analysis, focusing on objectivity and detachment. An individual who is high in feeling bases conclusions on personal feelings or social values, focusing on harmony and understanding.

Judging and Perceiving (J/P) describe how people deal with the outside world. An individual who is high in judging prefers to be decisive and seeks closure, dealing with the outside world using thinking or feeling. An individual who is high in perceiving prefers flexibility and spontaneity, dealing with the outside world using sensing or intuition.

From the four dichotomies come sixteen possible types. Each one of these types results from one pole of each of the four dichotomies, and each dichotomy is independent from the others.

From the MBTI, psychologists have created various ways to view personality in business. One such method is to consider the interaction or communication styles of various personality types. Although it is impossible to get individuals to take a personality test or reveal their personality style, you can study these personality types and learn how to detect most of these personality styles.

Another way to consider communication styles is to look at them from the psychological viewpoint and to classify individual communication styles — aggressive, passive, passive-aggressive, and assertive.

Aggressive communicators are brutally honest, direct, and forceful. They believe in win-lose situations (that is, they want to win and they do not care if you lose); this causes them to put down others so they can make their point or win the discussion. They prefer to make decisions and do not want to be corrected, even if they are wrong.

Passive communicators are inhibited, indirect communicators, fearful of offending, and prefer that others make the decisions. They are considered as "pushovers" by others, and they seldom get their communications needs met; they take a lose-win attitude to communication (that is, "I lose and you win").

Passive-aggressive communicators are manipulative and indirect. They will agree with you to your face, and later speak negatively about you with others. Passive-aggressive individuals make others feel confused, frustrated, and not sure what to expect from communications. They prefer to avoid problems rather than confronting them.

Assertive communicators are direct, honest communicators; they take a win-win attitude to communications ("I win and you win"). They treat others with respect but they have confidence in their own ability to communicate and come to agreement. They are willing to compromise and negotiate.

Intercultural Communications

Because of the global nature of business in the 21st century, you will most likely be involved with presenting business proposals to individuals in various countries and cultural situations. When communicating inter-culturally, remember that most communication problems come from the assumption that others hold mutual values, beliefs, and attitudes. Here are some principles to consider in these negotiations:

- Avoid using slang, jargon, clichés, and idioms (phrases unique to a particular culture that can cause confusion in your written business proposal or your presentation). For example, if you speak of someone getting his "just desserts," your listener may think you are talking about food. If you speak of "tearing your hair out," someone may think you are speaking literally.

- Listen carefully. Ask for confirmation. Do not assume you understand what the other person has said or written.

- Understand cultural differences in certain words and meanings. In some cultures, "yes," may not mean the same as it does in the United States. In some countries, for example, "yes" may not mean acceptance, but it may mean the other person is still willing to consider your proposal.

- Consider body language, spatial relationships, and other formalities. Some cultures shake hands, for example, while others would be offended if you did so. Presenting a business proposal in some countries may involve an extended period of informal discussion, and you may be considered rude if you immediately begin making your proposal.

The key to effective intercultural communication is prior study of the culture, patience, and an attitude of openness.

Increasing Readability

The subject of readability has been addressed elsewhere in this book, but it is important enough that it deserves a special mention.

Did you know that the average person in the United States reads at a fifth-grade level? The readers of your business proposal, most of whom have at least a high school education, will read at a tenth-grade level or higher. According to Doak, Doak, and Root (1996), legal and healthcare information should be presented at a seventh-grade level; some laws require that insurance information be presented at a fifth-grade level.

Be sure you understand the reading level of the audience to whom you will be presenting your business proposal. Several formulas and readability tests have been developed to determine the readability level of text. Here is a simple way to determine the reading level of a document, using the Flesch-Kincaid Grade Level score:

1. Select a writing sample between 100 and 125 words.

2. Determine average sentence length (ASL) by counting the number of words in each sentence and dividing by the number of sentences. Treat an independent clause (a stand-alone word group with a subject and predicate) as a separate sentence. For example, "In school we studied; we learned; we improved," would count as three sentences.

3. Determine the percentage of long words to obtain an average number of syllables per word (ASW). Count the number of words with three or more syllables. Omit proper nouns, combinations of short words (like butterfly), and verbs that gain a third syllable by adding "ed" or "es." Divide the number of long words by the total number of words in the sample.

4. Calculate the Flesch-Kincaid Grade Level score: (.39 x ASL) + (11.8 x ASW) − 15.59.

The easiest way to determine the readability level of your business proposal is to use the readability feature built into your word processor; most of the common word processing applications, including Microsoft Word, include this feature in the spell check and grammar programs. You simply check the "readability" index option in the preferences, and perform a complete spell check and grammar check of the document. At the end of this check, the readability information will be displayed. According to the Flesch-Kincaid Grade Level formula, the grade level for this book is 10.6.

As you can see, the best way to increase readability is to decrease the number of words per sentence and decrease the number of long words. If this advice sounds familiar, it ties in with the "7 Cs" section in Chapter 7, which also suggests shorter, simpler words.

Here are several other suggestions for increasing the readability of your business proposal:

- Increase the number of active sentences, while avoiding passive constructions. For example, instead of saying, "The proposal will be presented by several individuals," say, "Several people on our team will present the proposal." If you are not sure if a construction is passive, look for the word "by" and pay attention to where the action in the sentence is occurring; in active sentences, the person doing the acting comes first, followed by the action. Active constructions are not only easier to read, they also make sentences more personal and direct, and they increase the impact.

- Increase the number of concrete words while decreasing abstract ones. For example, instead of "office chair," use "executive chair" or "drafting stool." The more specific you can be, the greater the readability and the higher the interest level. Avoid abstractions like "progress" or "best." If you want to discuss how your product is the "best," talk about how it can benefit your client. Instead of saying, "We are making progress," state exactly where you are in your proposed timeline or what obstacles you are overcoming and when you expect to complete the work.

Increasing readability will increase the comfort level of your reader and the level of acceptance of your business proposal, so take the time to check the reading level of your document and make changes to increase readability.

You can also increase readability through the organization of your business proposal. A well-organized proposal has a linear message which proceeds from point to point from the beginning to the end. Good organization is important because:

- It helps your readers understand your message.

- It helps your readers accept your message.

- It saves your reader's time (which translates into saving money).

- It simplifies the communication process between you and the client.

A poorly organized business proposal, on the other hand, takes too long to get to the point, confuses the reader, and includes irrelevant material or material that the reader cannot find.

Group your ideas in a logical order. In a business proposal, you will proceed with a traditional proposal format:

- An executive summary, which provides an overview of the proposal

- An introduction to you and your company

- Background of the proposal

- A statement of purpose for the proposal

- The body of the proposal, proceeding from the statement of purpose

- A conclusion with your summation and request for the work

- A series of appendixes

The details of the organization of your business proposal will be discussed later in this book, but, for now, be aware that your organization (or lack of organization) will be a factor in gaining the acceptance of your clients for your business proposal.

Creating a Team Proposal for Business Clients

Sometimes you may need to work as part of a team to create a proposal in response to an RFP from a potential client. You will need to work with individuals from various departments to coordinate the efforts of several departments to make an effective proposal. Here is a case study from a proposal manager at a larger company who must put together just such a proposal:

CASE STUDY: PROPOSAL MANAGER

A proposal manager at a company serving the higher education market works with others to provide proposals to colleges and universities for administrative software and implementation and strategic consulting services, including student, financial aid, human resources, finance, alumni, portal, workflow, and other administrative products.

The process of presenting a proposal is as follows:

- An account executive identifies client needs and determines whether the company's products and services can fill those needs.

- A proposal analysis reviews the RFP.

- The products and services requested are identified.

- A strategic meeting is scheduled with the proposal response team (subject matter experts and management).

- An agenda is prepared for discussion at the meeting, highlighting all possible issues and questions.

- A workable project calendar is prepared, based on the project deadline.

- A work plan is prepared for the tasks, due dates, and participants.

The steps in planning a proposal include:

- The contents of the RFP are reviewed for a match to the products and services.

- The issues that would impede the response process are identified.

- The project calendar is built.

- The resources needed to respond to non-boilerplate requirements are identified.

- The outline of the response is developed based on the RFP requirements.

Before presentation, the document goes through multiple reviews by subject matter experts and individuals required to sign off on the business.

CASE STUDY: PROPOSAL MANAGER

To plan the proposal presentation:

- The proposal manager works with the sales team to understand the company's sales strategy.

- A pre-developed proposal template is used with descriptions of products and services, terms and conditions, and other related materials.

- The proposal presentation team works with sales and subject matter experts to understand the business requirements and to prepare customized responses where required.

The proposal presentation mirrors the format requirements of the RFP. The presentation is in Microsoft Word and uses graphics, pictures, and text. A hard copy is provided in a customized binder. Sometimes a CD or electronic e-mail version is included at the client's request.

Communication between various departments is necessary to prepare a top-quality proposal. Sales must provide a clear picture of the business strategy; the strategy cannot change in midstream, and the response team must fully understand the strategy.

The most effective proposals are those for which sales has developed a relationship with the client. It is essential to present a personalized proposal to address the client's vision and objectives by providing clear and direct benefit statements of the company's value, and understanding the client's goals and objectives. The proposal must show the client that their requests have been listened to. Avoiding boilerplate in key sales areas of the proposal is important to keep the proposal personal and increase its effectiveness.

Some advice from this experienced project manager:

- Qualify the account. If you are not the lead vendor, it is highly unlikely that you will win the business. Do not waste time and resources on no-chance proposals.

- Understand client needs, objectives and visions.

- Plan and coordinate your response prior to the release of the RFP. Work with sales support and other subject matter experts in supporting the process.

- Obtain buy-in from all participants before release of the proposal.

CHAPTER 5

SELLING YOUR PROPOSAL

Every business proposal involves selling. You cannot present the information in your proposal and sit back and wait for the client to say "yes" or "no." You must actively encourage the client to say "yes," and you must overcome client resistance. In other words, you must use the tactics of persuasion to obtain the "yes" on your proposal.

The principles of persuasion and selling are very old; in fact, they come from the Greeks and especially from the writings of Aristotle. In the second book of Aristotle's *Rhetoric,* he discusses the three means of persuasion for an orator. These persuasive methods can be adapted to any selling situation, including the presentation of a business proposal, so they are worth discussing.

The first persuasive method discussed by Aristotle is *ethos,* or credibility (translated roughly as "appearance" or "disposition"). Aristotle broadly described ethos to include not only moral character, but also expertise and knowledge. He mentions three categories of ethos (described below in the context of your business proposal):

- **Practical skills and wisdom.** You must persuade the audience that you have the skills and knowledge to fulfill the promises you make in the proposal.

- **Virtue, goodness.** You must persuade the audience that you are trustworthy and of good character, so they trust you to make good on your promises.

- **Goodwill toward the audience.** Establishing a relationship with your audience is the final factor related to ethos.

It should be noted that credibility is in the "eye of the beholder." If your client believes you are credible, then you are. It has been said that credibility is the most important form of persuasion, above the other two forms.

Credibility is the most important factor in the presentation of your business proposal. Your credibility is enhanced or diminished by the following factors:

- **Common ground.** You need to establish a connection or commonality of interest with your client at the beginning of your presentation. You can do this in a variety of ways. Some are simple techniques, while others take time. For example, express sincere appreciation for the hospitality of the company, noting little things like names of people. Take the time to learn a little about the individuals in the company, while not being too nosy. If, for example, you learn that a company executive likes to play golf, you can talk about this shared interest.

- **Your enthusiasm for the presentation.** You need to have a lot of energy and positive attitude in your presentation. If you go into the presentation of the proposal with little facial expression or if you show minimal enthusiasm, you will not be able to win over your client. After all, if you are not excited about the proposal, why should he or she be?

- **Your trustworthiness.** People are skeptical of salespeople, considering them low on the list of trustworthy professions. You need to overcome the skepticism by being honest and truthful with your client. For example, tell the truth about your product or service. If it is the most expensive on the market, talk about that, and explain how the price was determined and why it is of high value. If there have been problems with your customer service, explain what happened and what your company has done to fix these problems. Do not lie; do not skimp on the truth. Be direct and clear in your promises and show that you will keep them.

- **Your competence.** Competence is expressed in several ways:

  - **Your background, knowledge, and experience with the company and the products or services you are selling.** This is the reason you include a résumé with your proposal and begin with a discussion of your credentials.

  - **Your dress.** How you dress can affect how people think of you. Dressing tips for presenting proposals are discussed in Chapter 20.

  - **Your presentation's organization.** If you are organized in your proposal and the presentation, you show your client you are capable of handling a difficult and complex assignment easily. If you are disorganized, even if your disorganization has nothing to do with the actual presentation, you significantly lessen your credibility. For example, if you set up a PowerPoint presentation and your slides are out of order or if you have difficulty working the data projector, you will not win the confidence of your client.

The second persuasive method is *pathos*, engaging the emotions of the audience. You may think of pathos as something involving a strong emotion, but this concept also involves human interest and social proof. There are a variety of ways you can appeal to a business audience through the use of pathos:

- By telling a story about how previous clients used your product or service.

- By including testimonials and referrals in your proposal.

- By telling your reader success stories, to show this client the value of your product or service in his business.

Do not underestimate the value of storytelling and personal references in enhancing the sales value of your business proposal.

The third persuasive method is *logos*, which can be translated as "reasoning and logic." Most often it is described as an "argument from reason." Persuasion based on reason must be logical, using numbers, surveys, statistics, and other scientific or numeric data. To enhance your sales pitch using logos:

- Include visuals that show sales data and other statistics relevant to making your case.

- Include results from surveys or polls from other customers that can be used to show the value of your products or services. For example, if you can say, "73 percent of our present users rate our product as 'excellent' or 'above average' compared to other similar products," you are using a logical argument to persuade your client to accept your business proposal.

- Include opinions by experts in the field to support your propositions.

When you are using *logos*, or logical argument, to persuade your audience, be certain your sources are:

- **Relevant.** Use material that is "on target" with what you want to say. For example, if you are presenting a business proposal for a technical product, avoid using examples from a non-technical field. Your client will be more impressed with your proof if you stay within her specific field of knowledge.

- **Recent.** Avoid including material that is more than a few years old. The knowledge base changes every few years, and even something created just five years ago may be out-of-date by the time you present it.

- **Reliable.** Use only information from recognized sources. In some cases, your references may need to be from peer-reviewed journals. Be careful about using Internet resources, as many are unreliable for a variety of reasons.

- **Unbiased.** Many so-called "experts" have an agenda, or are trying to sell something.

Avoiding Logical Fallacies

Everyone is susceptible to being taken in by fallacies of reasoning, those statements that sound reasonable, but are not. A fallacy is a component of an argument that contains flawed logic. When you prepare your business proposal, you need to be aware of some of the most common logical fallacies so you can avoid using them in your writing and presentation. Here are some examples:

Ad hominem **argument.** This is an argument "to the man," which attacks an argument because of the person who is promoting it. "Nothing good can come from this person," is what an *ad hominem* argument states. *Ad hominem* arguments can also be against organizations; for example, "Microsoft is an evil company, so do not use its products." Poisoning the wells, or discrediting sources, is a variant of this argument.

Over-simplification. Political slogans are a good example of this fallacy, such as "Taxes are theft."

Appeal to (false) authority. Appealing to a legitimate authority is a good way to support your argument; using someone who has no authority is a different matter. For example, a creationist minister who discredited Darwin's theory of natural selection would be a false authority. Be sure your sources are legitimate authorities in their fields of study.

False cause. Assuming that because Event A came before Event B, it was the cause of Event B is a logical fallacy. Sequence is not causation. Because the rooster crows and the sun comes up, does not mean that the rooster caused the sunrise. Be careful not to attribute causation where none is there.

Generalization. This is the most prevalent type of logical fallacy; people generalize because they find it easy to assume a general rule from only a few cases. For example, if you go through a traffic light three times within a week and there is a police car there, you may begin to think, "The police are watching this light this week." That statement is a generalization. It may or may not be true; no one knows unless he watches the light all the time for a week to see if a police car is there. Generalizing about people is damaging; assuming that all people of a certain gender, nationality, sexual orientation, or race act in the same way can cause us to ignore the differences between people. Avoid generalizing about people and circumstances.

Argument from small numbers. This is a special case of generalization. The best example is flipping a coin. If you flip a coin 20 times and get 14 heads and 7 tails, your chances of getting heads or tails on the next flip is still 50/50.

These and other false arguments are often used in business and science. Be careful to avoid them in your proposal writing and discussions with clients.

Overcoming Resistance

When considering your approach to selling your business proposal to your prospective client, be aware that you may encounter various levels of resistance, from enthusiastic acceptance to downright antagonism. The approach you take must be tailored to the level of resistance you expect to encounter.

If you expect minimal resistance:

- Use a more direct approach in the presentation of your proposal.

- Identify with your client and establish the "common ground" discussed previously.

- Ask for the support of the client to help you win the proposal.

- If the client expresses approval, be sure to reinforce the correctness of the client's decision.

- Use logical argument to support your points.

If your audience is neutral:

- Begin your presentation by capturing the client's attention. Disinterest is more difficult to address than negativity. You must get the client away from indifference, and encourage the client toward enthusiasm and acceptance of your proposal.

- Start by establishing "common ground" by stating shared beliefs and values.

- Relate the proposal to the best interests of the people in the company or to the client's customers, depending upon which is most applicable to the situation.

- Be realistic about what you can do in one proposal. If you have not met with this client before your proposal, you may have to establish a relationship with the client before you can get the client to accept your proposal.

If your audience is negative or antagonistic:

- First, assume you can succeed in winning the client to accept your proposal. If you assume the positive, you have a greater chance of succeeding.

- Be indirect in your presentation. Do not announce your intention.

- Establish areas of agreement, even if there are only a few.

- Do not expect a major shift in the client's position with only one visit; use the first presentation to lay the groundwork for future presentations and proposals. It may take several presentations before you can win over the client.

- Acknowledge negatives and opposition. Answer the unanswered objection. For example, if you are making a presentation on a new product that is untried, acknowledge that the product has had limited testing, but the performed tests show marked improvement in productivity. If you do not acknowledge the unasked questions and concerns of the client during your presentation, they will remain in the person's mind and you will not be able to succeed in overcoming them.

- Work carefully to establish your credibility using the methods described previously. This may be the most important tactic for winning over a client.

The final factor that needs to be discussed in selling your proposal to your client is the ending of the presentation or the written proposal. The ending is the most important part in presenting your sales proposal. The most successful salespeople know the secret to getting their proposals accepted: Ask for the sale.

If the secret to success is asking for the sale, why do all salespeople not simply do it?

1. **Fear of rejection.** Many people have a fear of rejection; they feel rejected when someone says "no." Even in a business situation, people take rejection as a personal insult. The way to get past this feeling is to remind yourself that the rejection is not about you, it is about the client. The client is not rejecting you personally; he is rejecting this particular proposal. In another circumstance (for example, a different part of the company's fiscal year) or with a different person as decision maker, or even a different day of the week, your proposal may be accepted. The best way to handle fear of rejection to keep a positive attitude, and do not take the rejection personally.

2. **Inexperience.** The more times you ask for a sale, the better you will become at listening to client objections and overcoming them, and the more comfortable you will be with the asking. In your career, there will be many opportunities to "ask for the sale;" take advantage of every opportunity. If you are starting your career, look for opportunities to put yourself in the position of asking someone for something. Ask for a raise; ask for a special favor; ask for additional time off. The more you ask, the more comfortable you will be with the process.

3. **Not knowing how to ask.** New salespeople often are reluctant to ask for the sale, because it sounds intimidating and they do not understand that there are a variety of ways to structure the "close." A few of these techniques will be discussed below.

4. **Lack of a clear strategy.** If you go into a business proposal presentation without a clear understanding of what you expect the client to do, you will not be able to ask for it. When you are planning your proposal and presentation strategy, establish clearly what you want the client to do at the end. Do you want an order for a certain quantity of products? Do you want the client to sign up for your services? If the client has presented an RFP, it may make your planning easier, but you may also want to expand the RFP to include additional services or a longer time period. Spending time clarifying your strategy will make asking for the sale easier.

So you have decided you need to "ask for the sale." How do you go about it? Here are some suggestions:

- **Simply ask.** At the end of your presentation, say, "We would like your business. May we have your commitment to accept our project?"

- **Ask clearly.** Make your request clear and unambiguous; do not assume the client knows what you want. For example, if you say, "Are you ready to begin," your client may think you want to begin negotiations, while you may mean you want to begin working on the project or product.

- **Include a time frame with your request.** A good example is, "We can deliver the office system within six months of a signed contract. I have a contract with me today. May we get your signature on the contract so we can have the project finished by November 30?"

- **Assume acceptance.** Many sales people have learned the technique of asking, "Would you like this delivered by next Friday?" Another variation of asking with an assumption of acceptance is to ask about quantity: "Would you like 1000 or 2000 delivered?" Find a way to get the client to commit to the next step after the "yes." This is not a trick; it is an accepted way to turn prospects into buyers.

- **Avoid the aggressive approach.** Berating or lecturing to your client will not get you the sale. In fact, it may turn off the client to the point where you lose the sale. Using phrases like, "You need to do this," or "You should buy our product," are too aggressive.

- **Be politely persistent.** Keep asking until you get to the real objection. Often, it will take some digging to get to that point. For example, the client's budget may not allow the purchase, but he may be reluctant to express this in a group of subordinates. If you feel the client is reluctant to talk about the real reason for the objection, see if you can get the client aside to discuss it with you one-on-one.

- **Be ready with answers to objections.** Be prepared by taking the time to list all possible objections, including the most common ones like budget and timing. Being forewarned, in this case, is being forearmed.

- **Going back to the first suggestion, just ask.** You do not get what you do not ask for. Expressed another way, you lose 100 percent of the sales you do not ask for.

Building a Relationship with Your Client

Homer is quoted as saying, "The persuasion of a friend is a strong thing." In your work preparing for the presentation of your proposal, considering how to establish a good working relationship with your client is crucial. While there is a fine line between a working relationship and a personal relationship, you need to avoid crossing that line.

Establish a working relationship by spending time with the client, perhaps over a cup of coffee or lunch. Learn about that person's personality, goals, dreams, and professional expertise. This time should not be spent solely with the aim of using this information, but rather to form a professional friendship that will serve you well when you come to the table and present your proposal.

Establishing Your Credibility

Before you present your proposal, you must win the right to make the proposal in the first place. In the same way you must establish your credibility when you are speaking before an audience, you must establish your credibility before the audience to whom you are writing. For your proposal to be taken seriously and for your information to be considered for action, you must build credibility into every section of your business proposal. Credibility is built up in layers, from the most basic to the most complex. This section provides you with information about the layers of credibility you must include in your proposal.

Layer One: Your Personal Credentials

Before you can be taken seriously, you must establish the most basic level of credibility by telling the audience who you are and why you are qualified to write about the subject.

You must establish this basic credibility from the very beginning — in the introduction to the business proposal. In the introduction, include a section introducing you and your company.

Include awards and recognition, education and experience, published reviews, and testimonials from former satisfied clients (be sure to get approval). Include résumés of key people within your organization; give a brief biography of these people in the body of the report and point your reader to the complete résumé in an appendix. Do not overload this section with too many examples. For example, one excellent review by a client in the same field who has had an excellent experience with you is more valuable than several so-so reviews.

Layer Two: Your Understanding of the Basic Needs and Requirements of the Audience

You must show that you know what your audience is looking for. Create a client-centered message that clearly communicates your understanding of the client's needs. For example, suppose the client has stated that cost is a major factor in the decision to purchase your products. If you show the client the most expensive line of products, you lose credibility. On the other hand, if you explain that you know the client wants to look at lower-cost alternatives, you gain credibility.

Show that you have taken the time to get to know the client before you write the business proposal. Talk about the information you have gathered from the client during your discussions, and show how you have incorporated this information into your business proposal. Be clear about your intent to provide the service your client wants.

Layer Three: Evidence for Your Proposition

Depending upon the type of presentation you are making, you may need to include different types of evidence for your proposal. Here are some examples of evidence needed to substantiate a proposal:

- If you are preparing a proposal to take to a bank for a business loan, you may need to find evidence that you have a market for your products or services. In other words, you will need to prepare a demographic analysis of the population in the area you will be serving.

- If you are preparing an advertising proposal for a client, you may need to show the results of case studies or focus groups to show your client that your test campaign was successful.

- If you are proposing that a client purchase your services, testimonials from previous clients are helpful.

Here are some types of evidence you may use:

- **Case studies.** A case study is a type of qualitative experiment in which the researcher looks at just one instance or case. Sometimes a case study is used to disprove a theory which proposes a negative. For example, if a theory states there are no homeless people who have cell phones, a case study of one homeless person with a cell phone would disprove the theory.

  In most instances, a case study is used to gather information about an individual person or company or organization where there are many types of data that could be obtained and many sources of the information. A common type of case study is the business case in which a business is profiled and discussed by students in a management class as a teaching method. In a business proposal, a case study of how a previous client used your product or service may be helpful to get the prospective client to understand its usefulness.

- **Results of experiments.** Research experiments come in a variety of forms, but they revolve around the classic study called the "randomized clinical trial" or RCT. RCTs are considered highly reliable because they are structured to eliminate bias and control for variables.

  In an RCT, the primary investigator first isolates only one variable to study. Then she selects two groups: one is the study group and the other is the control group. The research is performed in a "double blind" manner; that is, neither the researchers nor the subjects know which group they are in. RCTs are used in medical, health, and pharmaceutical fields. For example, an RCT may be used to test the efficacy of a new drug. One group, the study group, receives the drug, while the control group does not. Results are analyzed to see if there is a positive correlation (relationship) between the use of the drug and improvement in the condition. Discussion of the results of an experiment such as an RCT is useful in a business proposal in which a company is promoting the use of a product that could be studied in this manner.

- **Focus groups.** Focus groups are formed to provide input about many subjects. The traditional focus group is composed of six to ten people, with a facilitator guiding the discussion and a note-taker or recorder keeping track of what has been discussed. Focus groups are used by marketers to gauge the acceptance of a potential new product, and they can also be helpful for small businesses wishing to improve their customer service. To be useful, the focus group should be carefully planned, with potential questions laid out in advance and the facilitator scripting the session.

The results of focus groups can be useful if you are presenting a marketing proposal to a client or if you are attempting to show a client that his business has a problem that you can help solve. In some instances, focus groups are part of a process of gathering information prior to the actual business proposal.

- **Success stories and testimonials.** Using success stories or testimonials about your product or service is a great way to show your client the value of your business proposal. They also add interest to your presentation. If you want to make a good impression, include short testimonials as evidence of your ability to please clients. Use success stories to show your prospective client how others have benefited from using your product or service. This type of evidence is helpful when you are discussing a service you have provided, since people who are skeptical about an unknown provider can be persuaded by social "proofs" like these. If you intend to use a success story or testimonial, be sure to obtain permission from the person or organization beforehand.

- **Expert testimony.** To add weight and credibility to your proposal, consider using the opinions of experts in your field. These experts should have the appropriate credentials, and these credentials should be recognized by the client to whom you are presenting. For example, if you are presenting a proposal for a "green" engineering project using environmentally friendly products to a client, using an expert on these products can help make your case for their use.

- **Surveys.** You can conduct your own surveys using online survey tools like Survey Monkey (**www.surveymonkey.com**) or Zoomerang (**www.zoomerang.com**). If you have time, you can conduct a mail survey to gain information for your proposal.

Layer Four: Your Persuasive Powers

Include clear and specific descriptions of the results your client will achieve. Present a recommendation that will solve your client's problem and will achieve specific and measurable results, including profit and productivity. Be certain that your proposal answers the question, "Why should I choose your proposal?" You must be convincing in your persuasion and in your proofs of superiority.

Persons reading or listening to your business proposal have three things they want to know:

1. **Is this proposal what I need?** Often, a company will come into a business to deliver a proposal based more on the ability of the proposing organization than on the needs of the company asking for the proposal.

2. **Can they deliver on their promises?** You need to convince the client not only of your ability to provide the products or services you propose, but also your ability to be available to answer questions and concerns on an ongoing basis. With proposals, you cannot only

describe the product or service; you must be clear about your ability to continue in the relationship. Setting up a service and support plan for a client can mean the difference between getting your proposal accepted or not. Here are some questions to ask yourself:

a. How will I describe my initial services, including installation and setup or the beginning of a service project? You must have a clear plan for the beginning of the project, including a delivery date and specific elements of setup and initial training, if necessary.

b. How will I describe my ongoing services to this client? Do you have a toll-free number that the client can call for service and support? Do you need to have an operator available at all times for this client, or will you be able to service the client's needs during regular business hours? What other types of service will you provide to assure that the client is completely satisfied?

3. **Is this proposal the client's best value?** Consider your client wants to get the best product or service available, and at the best price. The best product, if much more expensive than other proposals, may not be the best value. On the other hand, if you present a "low ball" bid within your proposal, and you find you have to go back to the client and add costs, you have lost your credibility. Determining your best price while creating value for your client is a tricky balancing act. Here are some tips:

a. Establish the lowest price you can afford for the proposal, considering all of the elements and components.

b. Add 20 to 25 percent to this amount. This is the offer to present to the client, giving you some bargaining room. If you make your proposal with your lowest amount, you have no "wiggle room" if the client wants to negotiate.

    c. As an alternative, you could present a high offer and work down from there.

Here are some other questions you should consider when establishing your credibility with your client:

- How do I want the decision maker to see me and my company? Whatever you do in your business proposal, you are creating an image of yourself and your company. Be certain of all of your statements; each one should work to promote the image you want to create.

- Does the client have previous experience with me and my company? Do they have previous experience (positive or negative) with my competitors? If you have been working with a client, you may have a lot of built-up credibility. You can capitalize now on the credibility you have built up in the past.

- Whose products or services is the client currently using? Mine? My competitor's?

- Am I providing specific recommendations for the client as part of this proposal? For example, if you were writing the proposal for office copiers described previously, you should include details about the machines you are recommending.

Here are some examples of nonspecific and specific language. In each case, you can see that the specific example is more believable, more interesting, and more persuasive than the nonspecific examples.

Version A (nonspecific): Our products are the most reliable in the industry.

Version B (specific): Our products have the lowest failure rate at 0.03 percent, with a mean time between failures of 1500 hours, the lowest in the industry.

Version A (poor): "Our service professionals are here to provide fantastic support for you."

Version B (better): "Our service professionals are available at all times at the toll-free number listed. Our Level One technicians speak English as their first language, and they have received 2000 hours of training in all aspects of our products. Our records show that 87 percent of questions are answered with one phone call." Being specific with your presentation adds to your credibility. Do not hesitate to add details; you can always take them out later if it is not needed. Most clients appreciate specifics.

Establishing Credibility Using Cover Letters

Some experts suggest that you include a cover letter with every business document you send. In a longer proposal with an executive summary, a cover letter may not be necessary, but it should be included in a shorter proposal, a letter proposal (see Chapter 14 for a discussion of letter proposals), or an informal proposal. Here are some tips on writing a great cover letter to enhance your credibility:

- The purpose of your cover letter is to entice the reader to read the proposal, not to present the entire proposal. It is primarily a sales letter, not the proposal itself.

- Start with a direct, friendly sentence or two to describe why you are writing. Do not be afraid to begin with a request for the work. For example, "Cosgrove Accounting Services is writing to request acceptance of our proposal for accounting services for Smith Manufacturing."

- Include a brief overview of your company and its capabilities. Point the reader to specific points in the proposal (using page numbers) and to your résumé or bio.

- Describe skills and abilities that make you and your company the best to do the work. Make this section different from the average cover letter. Avoid clichés and trite phrases such as, "We are a people-oriented organization."

- Close by describing your timeline and any other details requested by the client. Include contact information and the best time to reach you. Ask specifically for the work.

- Keep you cover letter to one page or less. People stop reading at the end of a page.

Preparing and Presenting Your Résumé to Enhance Your Credibility

A great résumé should be part of every business proposal, both to establish or enhance your personal credibility and to enhance your company's expertise in the mind of the client. You can create a run-of-the-mill résumé, or you can work a little harder and create one that stands out as exceptional. Like the cover letter, a résumé is a sales document designed to present your credentials in the most appealing manner possible.

As you consider how to structure your résumé, consider that there are two basic types of résumé formats: the chronological format and the functional format. A chronological résumé lists your education and your experience, both in reverse chronological order (that is, the most recent items first), while a functional résumé emphasizes the types of positions you have held and your skills and abilities.

An example of a chronological résumé may include the following headings:

- Education (above high school) and Special Training

- Professional Experience (listing companies in reverse chronological order)

- Skills and Abilities

- Awards and Honors

- Professional Affiliations

A functional résumé may includes the following headings:

- Summary of Experience — A short paragraph summarizing the person's qualifications, and highlighting those relating most closely to the present situation.

- Education, Professional Affiliations, and Awards and Honors, listing the most relevant items to the situation.

- Professional Experience, listed functionally, not chronologically.

- Previous Experience, listed in chronological order (in some functional résumés).

Here are some points to consider as you prepare your résumé:

- Use the journalistic technique of pyramid writing to put the most important information first. The most important information is a listing of skills and abilities. Within each section, list items in reverse chronological order — the most recent first.

- Many résumés include an "objective," which is a statement about the type of position for which the person is applying. If you are preparing a résumé to include with a business proposal, remove any previous objective that does not relate directly to this proposal, or create a new one that is specifically written for the occasion.

- Create an introduction that emphasizes the special skills and abilities that make you stand out and that provide your client with the confidence that they are making the right choice. In the introduction, use bullet points for these highlights and include a specific example of each one. A professional graphic artist, for example, might include the following highlight:

> **Deadline driven, punctual, and conscientious about project guidelines.** I follow your directions and deliver what you require.

- Tailor the résumé to the specific proposal being written. A general, nonspecific résumé does not produce the same results as one that has been directed to a specific audience. For example, if you have a variety of skills and experience in several different areas, emphasize those areas that best fit the kind of work you will be doing for the client. Consider the case of a graphic artist who may have done work for both a computer company and an educational software firm. If his next proposal is in the educational area, he should put that previous experience first in the résumé.

- Do not include personal information in a résumé; keep the résumé focused on your professional background. Information about your family, age, hobbies, and religious affiliations has no place in a professional résumé. Let the personal details flow naturally from the relationship and conversations with the client.

- Do not worry about keeping the résumé to one page; if you have followed the pyramid format of putting the most important information first, you will be accomplishing your goal of attracting the attention of your reader.

- Keep the format simple and professional; do not get caught up in fancy fonts and special templates. These extraneous factors may distract your client, and they may cause the client to miss your important qualifications.

- Include all relevant information about previous work positions:

  o Month and year you started at that position to month and year you left

  o City and state (city and province, or city and country) where the business is located

  o A brief description of the company, if it is not obvious or easily recognizable

  o Details about the work you did and accomplishments you attained at the position

  o Name of supervisor, if that person is still working for the company and is willing to provide information about the work you did for that company

If you worked at several different positions within a company, list the last or most senior position first.

- Include information about your professional affiliations, past and present volunteer activities, and organizations to which you belong. If you are a member of a national professional or leadership organization, such as Toastmasters or Rotary, list that information. Including this information is helpful in adding to your credibility as a professional, even if the organization or affiliation does not relate directly to the work you are doing for this client.

- After you complete the résumé, carefully review the entire document checking for errors in grammar, punctuation, and word usage. One error in a résumé can destroy the credibility you have so carefully built up with your client.

Items you should not include in a résumé include:

- Information on salaries or wages from previous positions.

- References from previous employers or clients. Add references in a separate document, usually as an appendix to the business proposal.

- Personal information, including marital status, number and ages of children, religious affiliation, hobbies, and recreational pursuits.

If you have not written a résumé recently, you need to spend time gathering the information and writing. The process of writing a résumé includes the following activities:

1. Collect all the data, including starting and ending dates of positions, names and titles of supervisors, and dates you received degrees or awards. This will take the most time because you may not have kept track of all of these pieces of information. If you cannot find an exact date, come as close as you can to the date. Do not make up information; if someone checks and finds incorrect dates, your professional credibility will be jeopardized.

2. Find a résumé format you like. If you use Microsoft Word, you may want to check out the templates that are included with the software or are available online. Check on the Internet for résumé formats.

3. Insert the information into the résumé and format it based on the résumé type (chronological or functional) you have chosen to use.

4. Proofread and review the résumé carefully. It is best to print out the résumé and look at it in printed form, rather than on a computer screen. Ask someone else who has good writing skills to review and proofread for you.

5. Print the final version on good paper. The paper does not have to be watermarked or cost a lot of money; good quality copy paper is acceptable for résumés.

Formatting Your Résumé

Here are some suggestions for creating a professional-looking résumé:

- Find or create a simple, easy-to-use format.

- Select a font and stick to it; mixing fonts in a document looks amateurish.

- Choose a serif font for easier reading (like Times New Roman, or Book Antiqua). A serif font has details and smaller strokes at the end of main letter strokes, as opposed to sans serif fonts like Arial. Serif fonts are easier to read in blocks of text.

- Make sure the font is big enough. Many common formats use at least 11 point font for the body of the résumé and 14 point font for section headings.

- Highlight section headings and key pieces of information with boldface type to make them stand out.

- Use underlining and italics sparingly, if at all.

- Do not skimp on the margins and the spaces between sections. Page margins should be at least one inch, and the top margin should be one and a half inches. Double space between sections and between bullets.

- Single space within listings (for each employment item, for example). This technique helps the reader see the pieces of information as separate and distinct, and breaks up the information into discrete sections.

- Use a "ragged right" format; do not try to use a fully justified format.

- Use bullets to set off items in a listing. Keep the length of bulleted items to three lines or less, so they "sell" your key points more effectively.

- Keep line lengths short. Studies have proven that it is easier to read information that is laid out in a long block of copy with shorter lines than a short block of copy with longer lines.

- Make sure you are consistent throughout the résumé with line spacing, headline treatment, and listing treatment.

- Use section headers. The section headers should all be the same size and font, and major words should be capitalized. For example, your sections may be:

  o Education

  o Skills and Abilities

  o Professional Experience

  o Awards and Honors

- Use the features of your word processor to create a header, with your name and page number on each page. Do not try to set up the header manually; you will spend too much time trying to re-do the headers as you make changes in the document.

- Lead your reader through the résumé. If the résumé is more than two pages long, add the word "continued" at the ends of pages.

- Use neutral-colored paper. Select white, off-white, ivory, or buff-colored paper for your résumé. These colors not only ensure readability, they are the least likely to prompt personal bias. Use a good quality, medium weight (20#) paper.

- Print on a good printer. Use a laser or good inkjet printer with a new ribbon. If you are making copies of the résumé, use a commercial copy shop for this purpose, or print all originals from your printer.

- Use the KISS principle — Keep it Short and Simple. Say as much as you need to say, and no more.

- Proofread. This point cannot be stated too many times; if your résumé is not error-free, you completely negate any goodwill built up with a client, and an error in a résumé could mean the difference between getting the proposal accepted or having it rejected.

- Make certain the résumé is flawless.

When you have completed your résumé following the suggestions here, you will have an excellent document to give to your clients to show them your capabilities and build your credibility as someone who has both the education and experience to succeed in the project described in the business proposal.

CHAPTER 6

SELLING POINTS AND VALUE STATEMENTS

By this point, you have spent a good deal of time thinking about your proposal, and you are ready to begin writing. Before you start the writing process, there are three things you need to do:

1. Create a value statement for your proposal, as described below.

2. Create your unique selling proposition.

3. Study the business proposal writing process described later in this chapter so you will have a clear sense of the tasks you need to complete, and the timeline you need to create to be successful in writing your proposal.

The Principles of Value

As stated in the previous chapters, successful business proposal writing has much to do with understanding the client and his needs, personality, knowledge, interest level, and level in the organization. From your reading so far, you should have some thoughts about how your proposal can provide value to the client. To understand the concept of "value," there are several economic principles that you can learn about.

The first is the principle of opportunity cost. Expressed most simply, the opportunity cost of any decision is the cost of the next-best alternative that has been foregone in accepting that alternative. Opportunity cost can be contrasted with accounting cost, which represents purely monetary cost, including such elements as depreciation. An example of opportunity cost may be a situation in which a business must decide whether or not to build a new building; in this case, the opportunity cost comes into play because the business will need to get a loan for the construction, and will not be able to use that loan for other purposes.

As you consider opportunity cost, be aware that, for your client to select your proposal, he or she is giving up the opportunity to select another proposal. Your proposal must be the best of the available proposals. This is where the second value concept comes into play: the principle of cost/benefit analysis.

Cost/benefit analysis is an economic tool that looks at the cost of a project compared to its perceived benefit. Sometimes cost/benefit analysis is a formal process done by an accounting department or financial analyst, in which the costs are spelled out against the future benefits of the action. In deciding whether to accept a proposal, your client may be looking at all of the costs included in the proposal against the benefit of the proposal. For example, if you are presenting a proposal for an advertising campaign, your client will be looking at the total cost of your services against the revenue it hopes to generate from the campaign.

For your proposal to be accepted, you must show that it contains a sufficient amount of value to your client. In other words, the opportunity cost of your proposal must be high enough to override other proposals or other uses for the client's money. To put it another way, what your client is giving up to accept your proposal, and the value of your proposal must exceed its cost, in at least one measure. Some methods for measuring the concept of "value" in a business situation are discussed below.

There are several ways that businesses consider the concept of the "value proposition," or the benefits the client receives in return for the money it expends. This section discusses the various areas in which your proposal may provide value to your client. Study this section and see how your proposal may fit into one of these categories and how your proposal may be accepted over the proposals of your competitors. The proposal with the highest value proposition wins.

- **Financial Value.** The financial value of your proposal to a client may include:

  o The lowest cost to purchase your product or services.

  o The lowest cost of operations. For example, your copiers may be less costly in terms of cartridges or cost of maintenance plan.

  o The greatest increase in revenue. Your proposed advertising campaign may provide the client with the highest revenue.

  o The greatest increase in per-item sold, which is similar to the increase in total revenue.

  o The greatest increase in customer base. If your proposal relates to Internet marketing, for example, you may be able to show the client that your search engine optimization (SEO) campaign will increase the number of "hits" on the customer's Web site.

- **Internal and External Social Value.**

  o Internal social value relates to increased employee satisfaction, and increases from training of employees and better employee performance. You may be able to show, for example, that your customer service training program will increase employee skills in dealing with customers.

o External social value is related to customers, including increases in customer loyalty, improved brand image and customer recognition, and a more specific position or niche in the market. Showing that your ad campaign will result in increased customer recognition is a value proposition.

- **Quality.** Increased quality relates to:

o Increased reliability of products.

o Fewer customer complaints may be another value of your sales training program, as described above. In this example, you can see how one proposal may be of value in several different areas.

o Compliance with regulations or quality initiatives, such as ISO 9001. One example may be the value of your OSHA materials or your ability to help the business keep its ISO 9001 status.

- **Technology.** Many instances of technological value are possible. For example:

o Flexibility of operations may be increased with use of your products or services.

o Reduction of down time may be a result of the office machines you are proposing to a client.

o New features of your sales and collections software may provide a value to your client.

o Improved automation of client processes from the software mentioned above may also be a value to the same client.

- **Minimizing Risk.** You may be able to provide value in this area by:

    o Increasing the health and safety of employees through client use of your OSHA compliance software or your OSHA analysis.

    o Avoiding liability. You may be able to show that use of your compliance software can reduce the risk of liability.

- **Competitive Value.** You may be able to show that your proposal will allow the company to:

    o Stay competitive with others in the industry.

    o Move ahead in the market.

Creating a Value Statement

After you have taken notes on the value areas above, the next step is to work on a value statement for your business proposal that will incorporate the value your proposal will bring to your client. From the examples above, find several key value points and write brief descriptions of how each can benefit the client.

Provide specific supporting statements for your value statement. For example, if you are writing a proposal on SEO software, show specifically how your software has helped other clients achieve higher levels of customer interaction. Be prepared to substantiate your value statement and to defend it if questioned. If you cannot provide support for any part of your value statement, it may be better to drop it than to make unsubstantiated claims that may destroy your credibility with the client.

After you write your value statement and supporting evidence examples, you can begin the business proposal writing process and find ways to incorporate your value statement into the business proposal. Your value statement will become an important touch point in your business proposal, as it will be inserted at key points in the proposal to emphasize your position. As you write the business proposal, keep your value statement at the top of your mind.

Developing and Presenting Your Unique Selling Proposition

In addition to creating your value statement, you should spend time thinking about and developing your unique selling proposition or unique selling point (USP). The USP is a common marketing term describing what sets one company or product apart from others. A USP is unique and it is a point used to sell a product or service. One example of a USP for a product is illustrated by L'Oreal's slogan, "Because you're worth it." You can find many other examples of USP in the cereal aisle, where one cereal is differentiated from another based on packaging and demographics.

Developing your USP will help you as you write your business proposal, because it will give you a focus or theme for your format. The USP describes your company, your products, or your services in three key areas:

- Who you are

- What you do

- Who you do it with

Who you are describes your company itself. If you look at the example in the success story in Chapter 26, you will see that Jonathan Lazar has set his company apart from others by creating a USP of "excellent service" and being "happy to help." Since their design services are not easy to differentiate from those of other designers, focusing on their company's attitude toward customers is a good way to create a USP.

What you do describes your company's products or services. Think about what makes your product different from the product of another similar company. What makes your copiers different from other copiers? If you are selling a product sold by other companies, focus on your service. What makes your services of higher quality than those of your competitors?

Who you do it with describes your specific customer market. The concept of "market" includes demographics, such as age, sex, and family status. The market for Jonathan Lazar's design service, for example, would be chiropractic practices, but he could also expand his market to include other healthcare practices.

As you think about presenting your business proposal, spend some time thinking about and developing your USP so that you can use this concept as a theme throughout the document and the presentation. If you have time, take the USP concept to a designer who can use it to create a logo and other visuals to help you sell your USP to your clients.

Additional Thoughts about Your Audience

Many businesspeople neglect the process of analyzing their audience, and as a result, they find their proposal does not meet with the acceptance they expected. Performing an audience analysis is one of the most productive tasks you can accomplish before you start writing your proposal. Here are some additional thoughts for you to consider about your audience:

Audience Demographics

- Are your audience members alike or different? What are the differences, if any? What do your audience members have in common?

- What is the average age of your audience? What range of ages is represented?

- How would you describe your audience in terms of socioeconomic status? What socioeconomic levels are represented?

- What occupations are represented by your audience?

- What ethnic, racial, or cultural groups are represented by your audience?

Disposition Analysis

- What does my audience expect from this business proposal?

- What do I expect about my audience's attitudes toward me and this proposal? Will they be receptive, neutral, or negative? Will the attitudes be mixed?

- What interests and goals do the audience members have?

- What will motivate your audience? What are their general and specific needs relating to this proposal?

- What biases or preconceived ideas may your audience have about you, your organization, and this specific proposal?

Knowledge Analysis

- How much does the audience know about the subject of this proposal? What knowledge levels are represented by the audience?

- What new information about this subject would help your audience? How could they use this information? How would their knowledge or lack of knowledge help or hinder the success of your presentation?

- At what point will you be "talking over the heads" of your audience members with information that is too complex? At what point will you be "insulting the intelligence" of your audience members with information that is too simplistic?

- What questions will your audience have about this proposal?

Political Analysis

- What levels of authority will be represented in the audience for this proposal?

- Who is the decision maker (or group of decision makers)? Will this person or group be at the presentation?

- Is there a gatekeeper who may prevent you from giving your presentation, or who may keep the decision makers from hearing your presentation?

Carefully reading this section and considering all of the questions about your audience will help you to prepare for the writing and presentation of your business proposal. Spend the time to complete this section before moving on to the writing section.

CHAPTER 7

THE BUSINESS PROPOSAL WRITING PROCESS

After you receive a business proposal and before you begin writing, take some time to go through the process outlined below to ensure that your proposal will be of the highest quality and most likely to succeed. This process assumes you are part of a larger company, but it also can be implemented by a single individual in professional practice.

A. **Yes/No Analysis.** Analyze your ability to accomplish not only the proposal, but the delivery of the products or services requested. In some cases, you may decide not to accept the proposal. See Chapter 1 for a more complete discussion of the decision process involved in not going forward with a proposal.

B. **Client Analysis.** Spend time talking to or thinking about the client. In your client analysis, include the specific needs of the client in terms of personality, expertise and knowledge of the proposal subject, and your credibility with the client. All of these issues are discussed more completely in Chapter 4.

C. **Proposal Analysis.** Discuss or think about how you will prepare the proposal. You may want to brainstorm or engage in the creative strategies described in Chapter 10 as you begin this process. Here are some elements of this analysis that you should consider:

i. What is the client's problem or issue that needs solving or resolving? Review the client's original RFP or documents you collected in your preliminary discussions with the client, so you have a complete picture of the requirements of the proposal.

ii. What levels within the client's organization need to be addressed within the context of the proposal?

iii. What are some possible solutions to the client's problem?

iv. What qualifications and experience do you bring to the client's problem?

v. Why should the client choose you and your company?

vi. What specific value proposition will be emphasized in the proposal?

D. **Strategy Creation and Outline.** Finalize your preliminary work by creating an outline of the proposal in relation to your key strategy.

E. **Practical Considerations.** Before you create the proposal, there are a number of questions you need to answer about the process and the presentation. These considerations are more applicable to larger companies with several individuals involved in the proposal process, but even if you are a solo professional you should go through the thought process involved in this section:

i. Who will write the parts of the proposal? There may be several people in your company, some of whom have more expertise in writing different sections of the report. For example, your technical staff may need to write the more technical portions of the proposal, while you may want to write the executive summary yourself.

    ii. What visuals will be needed and who will be responsible for preparing them?

    iii. How will you present the proposal? What format will you use and what individuals will be at the presentation?

F. **Timeline.** Create a proposal timeline. The best way to do this is to work backwards from the required completion date. Creation of a proposal timeline is discussed more completely later in this chapter.

G. **Proposal Creation.** Write the proposal, including all sections and graphics.

H. **Review and Edit.** Ask several people to review the proposal document, each one with a specific task:

    i. One of these individuals should review with an eye to the "7 Cs," paying close attention to sentence structure, language usage, spelling, and typographical errors.

    ii. Another person should review from the point of view of the client who is unfamiliar with the subject of the proposal, to look for jargon or language that is unclear or overly technical.

    iii. A third person should look at the proposal from the point of view of a skeptical client who needs much persuading. The question this person should ask is, "Does this document make me want to accept the proposal?"

I. **Final Review and Preparation.** Before you send the proposal to be printed, spend time with your team or by yourself quietly reviewing the proposal, to make certain it contains everything you need to be successful, and nothing extraneous that will distract from your purpose. Leave sufficient time in your timeline for this important final review. See Chapter 27 for a list of final questions to ask before you print the proposal.

J. **Presentation Creation and Preparation.** The final portion of the process should be the development of the presentation with rehearsal and role playing. The process of presenting your proposal is discussed more in Chapter 20.

Creating a Proposal Timeline

As soon as you know the client's deadline for your proposal, you need to construct a proposal timeline. For simple projects, the construction of a timeline is a matter of simply recording the end date and considering the following dates leading up to it:

1. Record today's date as the beginning of the process (even if it is not the date you begin writing the proposal), since you will be starting the process today by thinking about what you will do and how you will work on this proposal.

2. Set out internal deadlines for the steps in the proposal writing process outlined above. Depending on how many people in your organization are involved, these steps may take more or less time. For example, doing a creative analysis of the client and the project may take several weeks if there are many people in your company who must come together for these discussions. For a solo practitioner, the analysis phase may take only a few days of concentrated thought and brainstorming.

3. Include time for careful review by anyone you feel can provide substantive input.

4. Include time for printing copies of the proposal.

5. Include time for preparation and rehearsal of the presentation.

6. Include time for the unexpected, like printer breakdowns, unavailability of key people in your organization, and general "Murphy's Law" type problems. No matter how carefully you plan, there will always be problems and delays, so do not be caught unaware at the end by not being able to finish before the deadline.

The 7 Cs of Successful Proposal Writing Style

You never know who will read your proposal. Some readers have little interest in grammar, spelling, courtesy, and conversational style. Others may have been English teachers in a previous career, or they may be analytical individuals who expect precision in everything. The point is, you do not know, so to be certain your style will be approved by your reader, you must adhere to these common principles of writing. As you write your business proposal and edit it after writing, keep the following seven principles of language and style in mind:

Clear Writing: To be clear, you must be incapable of being misunderstood. In other words, you must write so clearly that your reader, no matter what his reading level, will understand what you are saying. To write clearly:

• Use short words and short sentences.

• Use specific, concrete words instead of vague words.

• Avoid clichés, slang, and jargon.

• Avoid hidden verbs and passive constructions.

Concise Writing: Use the fewest possible words, both to avoid misunderstanding and to save valuable time for the reader and writer. To write concisely:

- Avoid redundancies, like "prior planning," and "cooperate together."

- Avoid meaningless "rubber stamp" phrases, like "pursuant to" and "enclosed herewith."

- Review your writing, looking for words you can cut without changing the meaning. It is easier to write many words than fewer words. You can often cut a sentence down by rearranging the words or cutting out redundant and unnecessary words.

Complete Writing: Complete writing includes making sure you include all relevant information and all relevant portions of the document. To make sure your writing is complete, ask, "If I were the reader, is there a question that I would want answered?" Ask someone else to read your business proposal before it is presented, and have that person ask the same question. If the reader has questions, you have not yet written completely.

Correct Writing: Correct writing is 100 percent perfect in grammar, spelling, punctuation, and usage. Correct writing also means that you use the correct format, including headings, subheadings, and margins. Using the correct word for the specific situation is also a mark of correct writing. To be certain your business proposal is written correctly:

- Proofread carefully. Read section by section, keeping in mind the overall point of each section.

- Use a style manual, spell check on your word processing application, and use other references. For this book, the Gregg Reference Manual was used. You can purchase a copy or use their online service and search for answers to specific questions you may have about usage. Use a current dictionary to check spellings and meanings of words. Several good online dictionaries are **www.dictionary.com** and Merriam-Webster (**www.m-w.com**). Keep one of these dictionaries bookmarked for quick reference.

- Ask someone to edit your proposal. Find someone who is good with these subjects and ask the person to read carefully, noting both the obvious errors and the more subtle usage and wording issues. Do not be offended by this editing; the more care you take now with this task, the less likely you will be to suffer criticism later from someone you want to impress.

- Be certain you are using the right word for the situation. Use the thesaurus built into your word processing program to look for synonyms. If you do not know the meaning of a synonym or understand the difference between words, stop and look up the word. For example, if you do not know whether to use "important" or "importantly," look them up. Spending time on these subtle but vital word choices can give you an advantage with readers.

Conversational Writing: To keep your writing conversational, write as if you were talking to the other person. Even if many people will be reading your proposal, you are only writing to one person at a time. Most business proposals are written in the third person, but you can avoid the stilted language that sounds like "legalese" by using the following writing techniques:

- Considering your reader as a friend, write as if you were sitting at a business dinner talking to this person.

- Avoid legal terminology. Some businesspeople think that legal words and phrases make a proposal sound more important and valuable; actually, these meaningless phrases often make the document impossible to read. Legal phrases have little place in an effective business proposal. Save the "whereas" and "pursuant to" phrases for the attorneys.

- If there is only one person who will see the proposal, you may want to address this person by name. Do not do this too often (you do not want to sound too chummy), but you could put the person's name at the beginning of the report, just to set a tone of friendship.

- Consider the level of formality of the report, and tailor your conversational style accordingly. In a casual report to a single individual, for example, you can be a little more conversational than in a formal report to a senior executive committee.

Courteous Writing: In every situation, treat the reader with courtesy. You are trying to impress this person, so you will be naturally courteous. Some pointers on courteous writing:

- Remember the Golden Rule, and treat others as you want to be treated.

- "Please" and "thank you" are always appropriate. Look for good places to include them.

Constructive Writing: Constructive writing creates a "win-win" dynamic between the reader and the writer. Write with the expectation that both parties in the proposal can achieve their objectives. As you write, think about how you can provide a benefit to your reader and to yourself. Learn how to be an assertive communicator, as discussed in Chapter 4.

Ten Ways to Improve Your Writing

Business writing styles tend to be formal and legalistic, as large companies rely on managers and corporate attorneys to formulate documents. Many people learned their business writing styles in these large companies, and they learned how to write formally and with an eye to legal issues. In recent years, small businesses have found that more informal and less legalistic styles are more accepted by clients. These new, more comfortable, friendly, and understandable writing styles are based on the "7 Cs" described previously. If you want to write better and have your business proposals and other business writing accepted and understood, here are ten tips to help you improve your writing:

10. Use short, familiar words and sentences.

9. Eliminate redundancy.

8. Be specific and concrete; use names, numbers, and dates, strong verbs and vigorous language.

7. Accentuate the positive; eliminate the negative.

6. Stamp out rubber stamps.

5. Avoid hidden verbs and other passives.

4. Avoid pompous language, clichés, slang, and jargon.

3. Use courtesy and avoid discrimination.

2. Be confident and assured, but not overly confident or pushy.

1. Write from your reader's point of view.

In More Detail

10. Use Short, Familiar Words and Sentences. Business writers seem to have the idea that using a big word is more meaningful or that big words are more important and businesslike. This is not true; small words are more understandable and make the reader more comfortable. Redundancies are also wasteful and meaningless. Keep your words and sentence short to increase understanding and to avoid wasting valuable reader time.

For example:

Instead of: We need your assistance.

Use: We need your help.

Instead of: Please endeavor to deliver promptly.

Use: Please try to deliver promptly.

Instead of: I hope you are fully cognizant of the implications.

Use: I hope you know the implications.

Instead of: I was unavoidably detained.

Use: I was delayed.

Instead of: I subsequently learned of the order.

Use: I later learned of the order.

Instead of: Inasmuch as you have met the managers . . .

Use: Since you have met the managers . . .

Instead of: It is probable that we will be ready to order.

Use: We will probably be ready to order.

Instead of: We need to wait until a later date to make this decision.

Use: We need to wait until later to make this decision.

Even better: We need to wait until we have established our budget for the year to make this decision. (This includes specific details and eliminates the need for more explanation of the word, "later.")

Shorten wordy phrases to make them easier to read and understand. In many cases, reworking the sentence also adds a more personal, conversational tone. For example:

Instead of: The financial advantage of owning this equipment is 15 percent after taxes.

Use: Owning this equipment will save you 15 percent after taxes.

Even better: You can save 15 percent after taxes on this equipment.

Instead of: Selection of an insurance company should be based on . . .

Use: Select the insurance company that will . . .

Note how the understood "you" helps make this second sentence more personal and direct.

Instead of: Keep this information on file for future reference.

Use: Keep this information for reference.

Instead of: The reason we are recommending this procedure is because

Use: We are recommending this procedure because

Note that the use of the personal pronoun "we" makes the sentence more personal, direct, and understandable.

9. Eliminate Redundancy. Avoid repetitive words and redundant expressions like the following and see how your writing is improved.

For example:

Instead of: These items are absolutely free . . .
Use: These free items . . .

Instead of: The price still remains $199.95.
Use: The price remains $199.95.

Instead of: Our customary practice is . . .
Use: Our practice is . . .

Instead of: We like to cooperate together with you.

Use: We would like to cooperate with you.

Instead of: We will meet at about 10 a.m.

Use: We will meet at 10 a.m.

Note that elimination of the word "about" also eliminates possible misunderstanding.

Instead of: The true facts in this case are . . .

Use: The facts in this case show . . .

Instead of: We seldom ever need to . . .

Use: We seldom need to, or We never need to . . .

Eliminate common unnecessary compound phrases such as:

- Part and parcel

- Pleased and delighted

- First and foremost

- Ready and willing,

- Prompt and immediate

8. Be Specific and Concrete; Use Names, Numbers, and Dates; Use Strong Verbs and Vigorous Language. Here are some examples to show the importance of being specific. The first instance in each pair is imprecise and vague; the second is specific and concrete. Note how the specific sentences use numbers, like "75 percent" and $99.56; names, like "Sam;" and dates, like "November 21" to provide the reader with more information and eliminate misunderstanding.

Instead of: We received a positive response.

Use: We received a 75 percent positive response.

Instead of: Please submit an invoice for the full amount.

Use: Please submit an invoice for $99.56.

Instead of: Sam received a low rating on his report.

Use: Sam received a rating of C- on his report.

Instead of: We traveled a sizable distance in a short time.

Use: Carolyn and I traveled 12,000 miles in six months.

Instead of: We need the money soon.

Use: We need the money no later than November 21.

Note how specifying an exact date, and the use of "no later than" avoids any misunderstanding about the due date.

Instead of: A high proportion of survey respondents visit the Web daily.

Use: Out of the 70 people surveyed, 25 visit the Web daily, a 35 percent rate of daily viewing.

In this case, you are creating a longer sentence, but it is more specific and provides the reader with more information.

7. Accentuate the Positive. Studies show that people respond better to positive phrases than negative ones. In customer service in particular, using positive phrases helps build a relationship with the client. Consider how the positive attitude in these examples could increase your ability to relate to the client:

Instead of: We hope you are not <u>dissatisfied</u> with our service.

Use: We hope you are satisfied with our service.

Even better: We work to make sure you are satisfied with our service.

Note that the second instance eliminates the double negative in addition to increasing positive feelings.

Instead of: We apologize for the inconvenience. We are sorry this happened, and we regret that it happened.

Use: Please accept our apology. The replacement should arrive no later than January 30.

Note that the second example includes a brief apology, which the customer expects, but then states specifically what will be done to resolve the issue. Avoid using the word "inconvenience" in these situations. This word gives a meaning of "minor problem," when it may be a major issue and a serious problem to the customer. Also note the use of three negative words: "sorry," regret," and "apologize." You should express your sincere apology, but state it once and let it go. Focus on the solution, not the problem.

Instead of: There has been a delay in our shipping. We have been having trouble with our shipping company.

Use: We have moved our shipping date to January 15, and you will receive your shipment no later than January 20.

Note that the second example provides the information the customer wants to know (when the item will be received), and it does not include the information the customer does not care about (the shipping problem).

Instead of: We are experiencing a problem with our quality control and our error rate has increased.

Use: This item slipped by our inspectors. We are sending a replacement, and we guarantee it will work as you expect.

Again, note the elimination of any mention of your company's problem. The key to eliminating these negative phrases is to think like a customer and ask, "What do I want to know?"

Here are some words you can use often, because they convey positive feelings. For example:

- Enjoy

- Success

- Fortunate

- Benefit

- Comfortable

- Encourage

- Pleasure

- Welcome

- Valuable

<u>Never</u> use the following words: "can't," "impossible," and "unable." There is always a way to work with the customer to satisfy her request and to provide a positive solution. In many cases, agreeing to do something if the customer does something in return is a good way to solve a problem. Find a positive way to write. Although it may take a little thought, you can avoid these words. Here are some examples:

Instead of: We <u>can't</u> send your item until after Christmas.

Use: You will receive your item by December 27.

Note that the word "can't" is negative, it is also an apology, and it is a statement of a past condition. The word "will" is future-directed and positive, and it tells the customer what he wants to know.

Instead of: It is <u>impossible</u> for us to make an exception for your situation.

Use: We would be able to do this if we have your approval to . . .

Note that you can almost always find a way to comply with the request of a customer if they agree to do something in return.

Here are some additional examples of negative phrases that can be turned into positive ones with a little careful thought:

Negative: I *do not* yet have any work experience.

Positive: My two terms as secretary of the Key Club have given me . . .

Note that in a resumé you should not lie, but you do not need to include negative information. Instead, focus on your experiences and qualifications.

Negative: You <u>neglected</u> to send the signature we need to process your request.

Positive: Please send a signed copy so that we can process your request.

Note that the phrase "neglected" put the blame on the customer and causes ill-will. It is better to state clearly what you want the customer to do.

Negative: We <u>apologize</u> for this error.

Positive: We appreciate you calling this matter to our attention.

Negative: We <u>are not</u> open after 7 p.m. on Fridays.

Positive: We are open until 7 p.m. on Fridays.

Negative: We received your <u>complaint</u> letter about our service.

Positive: We received your letter about our service. Thanks for letting us know about this item. We are sending a replacement, which will arrive by January 10.

Note that using the word "complaint" casts the customer in a negative light. The customer may feel that he or she has a legitimate issue with your service. Acknowledge that you have received the customer's letter and go on to state what you will do to solve the problem.

Negative: Do not send until you have signed . . .

Positive: Please sign and send . . .

Note that the first example demeans the customer's intelligence and ability to follow directions, while the second example is a clear statement of what you need the customer to do.

Negative: It is our policy not to allow...

Positive: We would be happy to pay this bill if . . .

Note that hiding behind "policy" is negative and causes customers to feel they have not been treated as individuals. The best solution for a situation in which you have rules is to state the reason as briefly and positively as possible. Then go on to explain the circumstances under which both of you can receive what you want.

Negative: The letter you claim to have sent has not arrived.

Positive: Your letter has not arrived.

Note that the first sentence sounds mistrusting and gives the customer the message that you do not believe him.

Negative: We must regretfully deny your claim.

Positive: Although this claim is not eligible for payment, we will pay future claims if . . .

Note that the phrase "regretfully deny" may not be believed. The second instance puts the emphasis of the sentence on what you can do in the future.

6. Stamp Out Rubber Stamps. "Rubber stamp" phrases are old and overused business cliché's that have little or no meaning, and which do not add to the sentence in a positive manner. Consider the following opening and closing phrases:

Instead of: Herewith enclosed please find . . .

Use: Enclosed is...

Even better: I have enclosed the . . .

Note that the last sentence includes a personal pronoun and results in a more conversational tone.

Instead of: Thanking you in advance for your assistance in this matter, I remain . . .

Use: Thanks for your help.

Note that the phrase, "I remain" is antiquated and it should not be used. To thank someone before they comply with your request is presumptuous. Just say thanks.

Instead of: If you have any questions or concerns, please do not hesitate to contact us.

Use: Let me know if you have questions or concerns.

Better: I look forward to helping you at any time.

Note that the first sentence contains the negative phrase "do not hesitate." This phrase is overused and it has lost its effect. The second sentence is more direct, but it still implies that the customer may have a problem, which has a negative feeling and is not the tone you want to take. The third sentence is positive, direct, and helpful.

Instead of: Advise this office ASAP if this is acceptable to you.

Use: Let me know if you agree with the terms of this contract.

Note that the phrase "this office" is meaningless and pretentious and it should be avoided. The acronym "ASAP" may not be understood by some readers, particularly those who are not native English speakers.

Instead of: Please reply at your earliest convenience.

Use: Please reply by January 15.

Note that the phrase "your earliest convenience" can mean anything from tomorrow, to three weeks from now, to never (if it will never be convenient). To make certain you receive a response when you need it, specify the date.

Instead of: Please acknowledge receipt of this letter.

Use: Please let me know by e-mail when you receive this letter.

Instead of: Please return to the undersigned in SASE.

Use: Please sign and return to me using the enclosed envelope.

Note that the term "the undersigned" is not common knowledge (it refers to the person writing the letter), so your reader may not know to whom you are referring. The acronym "SASE" may also not be understood. The fact that the envelope is self-addressed and stamped need not be mentioned unless there is more than one envelope enclosed.

Instead of: Enclosed please find letter of the 12th Inst. Pursuant to your letter of May 30th.

Use: I am writing in response to your letter of May 30.

Note that the first sentence is completely outdated and almost unintelligible, but some letter writers still use this type of phrasing. The phrase "Inst." refers to "this instance," or the date of the letter. Also note that the phrase "enclosed please find" is better stated by using a more conversational style, using personal pronouns.

5. Avoid Hidden Verbs and Other Passives. Hidden verbs are phrases that contain a verb form; they are stated more effectively by using the verb itself. For example, the phrase "come to a conclusion" contains a form of the word "conclude." It is always more powerful to use one word instead of many to say something. Passive phrases are those in which the person is acted upon rather than acting. If you are not sure what a passive phrase is, look for the word "by." For example, "The ball was thrown by Steve," is a passive sentence; the active version would be, "Steve threw the ball."

Active sentences are almost always more direct, personal, and positive. The only time you would use a passive sentence is to avoid blaming. For example: "The mistake was made by Purchasing," rather than stating, "Larry Smith made the mistake." Here are some examples of hidden verbs and passive phrases:

Instead of: I will make an adjustment to your bill.

Use: I will adjust your bill.

Instead of: Please make a payment on your account.

Use: Please pay on your account.

Instead of: The committee reached a conclusion yesterday. The group decided that . . .

Use: The committee concluded yesterday that . . .

Note in the first sentence it takes two sentences to get to the point of what the committee concluded, while in the second sentence, the critical piece of information about the decision is stated immediately.

Instead of: Please take this into consideration.

Use: Please consider this.

Note that in sentences like these, it is good to shorten the number of "filler" words so you can be more direct, as with the second sentence.

Instead of: The group held a meeting last Monday night.

Use: The group met last Monday night.

Instead of: The report was signed by Mary.

Use: Mary signed the report.

Note that in this instance, Mary is probably not in trouble for signing the report, and you are providing the customer with information about the person to contact for questions.

4. Avoid Clichés, Slang, and Jargon. In addition to the words and phrases mentioned above, there are several other specific types of phrases that you should avoid. The first kind of expression is the **cliché**, which is an over-used descriptive phrase that was interesting when first used but, which has lost its power. The expressions "raining cats and dogs" and "packed in like sardines" are examples of clichés.

The second kind of expression is **slang**, which is a casual conversational word or phrase that is trendy and often used by young people, but which is not intended for business situations. The expressions "awesome," "cool," and "dude" are examples of slang words.

The last kind of expression is jargon, which is specialized technical language and acronyms used by a specific trade or profession. Many of the expressions of the computer world, for example, are used more generally, such as "interface" or "hacker." Another example is the military and aircraft world, which uses expressions like "Roger" and "SNAFU." When you work in a profession, it is easy to get caught up in the terminology of that profession and to forget that others do not share in the understanding of that terminology. Jargon is easily misunderstood, particularly by people who are not native speakers of English or those who are not familiar with the terms. Avoid using jargon unless you explain the meaning of these terms. The following are some examples of cliché, slang, and jargon and how to avoid them.

Edit out clichés such as the following:

Instead of: It goes without saying that we are interested in the project.

Use: We are definitely interested in the project.

Instead of: I don't want to beat around the bush.

Use: I want to make my point clearly and quickly.

Instead of: I hope this is crystal clear to you.

Use: I hope this is clear to you.

Instead of: Last but not least, I am ready to begin the project.

Use: I am ready to begin the project.

Instead of: It is an unwritten law that . . .

Use: It is common business practice to . . .

Avoid industry-specific jargon, and terms that outsiders might not understand.

For example, in education, an "instrument" is a test. Someone who does not know this jargon may think of a musical instrument.

Medical workers also use jargon when talking with patients. For example, a doctor may talk about COPD, which is an acronym for chronic obstructive pulmonary disease. Even knowing the full wording may not be helpful for some people, and using "emphysema" also may not be helpful. It is best to say "lung or breathing disease."

A lot of jargon from the sports world has permeated the business world. Expressions like "carrying the ball," "keeping score" "end run," "play ball," and "home run" may be used in conversations with businesspeople who understand them, but they should not be used when writing business proposals.

Avoid slang expressions in favor of more businesslike ones.

Instead of: Our team has created an awesome proposal.

Use: Our business group has created an exceptional proposal.

Note that the word "team" comes from sports jargon and should be avoided.

Instead of: We have your back on this one.

Use: We will support you on this project.

Instead of: That was a sad presentation yesterday.

Use: That was a poor presentation you made yesterday.

3. Use Courtesy and Avoid Discrimination. Avoiding discourteous and discriminatory language was discussed in Chapter 2, but as a reminder, be sure to carefully scrutinize your business proposal to be certain it does not contain any such expressions or phrases. Even one such expression in a proposal can cause one of your readers to take offense, and it can limit or even destroy your opportunity for a success.

For example:

Instead of: We need to find the best man for the job.

Use: We need to find the best person for the job.

Instead of: All the executives and their wives will be invited to the open house.

Use: All the executives and their guests will be invited to the open house.

Note that using "guests" avoids discrimination and includes spouses, significant others, and those who would like to invite a special friend.

Instead of: My girl will take care of the flight arrangements.

Use: My assistant will take care of the flight arrangements.

Instead of: Each manager must evaluate his employees.

Use: Managers must evaluate their employees.

Or: Each manager must evaluate his or her employees.

Or: Each manager must perform employee evaluations.

2. Be Confident and Assured, but Not Overconfident or Pushy. It is difficult to find the right tone for business writing. Some proposal writers find themselves preaching to their readers. Others use a pushy style to make their points. Still others come across as bragging. As you write your proposal, be aware of your style and the way you sound to readers. Try to find a style that will be read as confident but not bragging, and that will sound self-assured and helpful but not pushy. Here are some suggestions to help you develop your style:

Avoid phrases like these:

- Firms like ours cannot survive unless clients pay their bills on time.

- You must not have read the directions that we gave for filling out the insurance forms.

- You are quite obviously a highly educated and self-aware person who appreciates the value of good connectivity.

- Your satisfaction means more to us than earnings and profits, and we shall work day and night to see that we earn it.

Replace: I know you are a busy person, but we would enjoy hearing you speak on . . .

With: We would enjoy hearing your speech on . . .

Replace: I hope you will agree that my qualifications match your job needs . . .

With: My qualifications match your job needs in the following ways . . .

Replace: If you agree, the bill will be turned over to our collection agency.

With: Unless we hear from you by November 14, we will turn the bill over to our collection agency.

1. Write from Your Reader's Point of View. Of all the tips listed here, writing from the reader's viewpoint is the most important. The best way to connect on a personal level with your readers and to give yourself an advantage in your business proposal is to present yourself as if you were talking directly to the reader. Adopt a tone of businesslike friendliness. Be careful not to become overly familiar (using slang, for example), but keep the stodgy and trite business phrases to a minimum. Here are some examples to illustrate the principle of writing from your reader's point of view:

Instead of: I am happy to be able to report . . .

Use: You will be happy to know . . .

Note that you are trying to get your reader to feel you have his interest in mind, and not your own. Starting sentences with "you" rather than "I" is a great way to do this.

Instead of: We are pleased to have you as a client.

Use: Welcome to Champion Services.

Note that sometimes it is effective to talk about "family," as in "Welcome to the Champion Services family." This depends upon the type of company, the situation, and the relationship that has been developed.

Instead of: Our massage therapist is highly qualified . . .

Use: You will feel more relaxed after ...

Note that you are emphasizing benefits to the client, not features that you are providing. For more information on this concept, see Chapter 4.

Instead of: To take advantage of this opportunity . . .

Use: You can take advantage of this opportunity by . . .

Note again that the word "you" starts the sentence. Finding opportunities to use this word will help you create the reader viewpoint. Another way you can do this is to create statements that read like commands, with "you" understood. For example, "Come to our open house . . ." is a command in which the word "you" is understood.

Choosing a Writing Style

You may have a particular style you like to use in writing, but consider that a business proposal should contain a more professional style of writing than other business writing, such as letters. In addition to some of the style considerations above, here are some suggestions for achieving a professional yet friendly writing style in your business proposal:

Mirror the client's style. If you have the client's RFP or other documents that set out the client's specifications and requirements, read through them carefully to get a sense of their writing style. Then copy the style in your own documents. Note how the client refers to himself. Many companies refer to themselves in capitals, such as "the group" or "the firm." Use the same references to the company in your proposal. If the client has a formal style, use a formal style; if they have a more casual style, use that style.

Refer to yourself as a team. Unless you are a solo professional, write as if all of the individuals who are participating in the proposal are one unit, Use the plural first person "we," "us," and "our." Do not refer to yourself in the third person unless you feel the situation demands it. Using a friendly personal style helps establish the relationship between you and your client.

Use positives. As described previously, positive statements are more effective. Use the "find/replace" feature of your word processor to search for instances of the words "not," "can't," "won't," "don't," and other common negative expressions, and change your wording to eliminate them as much as possible.

Express confidence, but avoid boasting. Use strong positive statements about your ability to fulfill the needs of the client. Avoid unnecessary negatives. For example, you may not have much experience with this type of work, but you do not need to say this. Instead, talk about the experience you do have, and what this experience enables you to do for the client. On the other hand, avoid boasting. If you include value statements, they should be supported by evidence. Unsupported statements about past achievements or empty promises can damage your credibility. A statement like, "We are available to our customers at all times" must be supported with testimonials and customer service reports to be credible.

Avoid overstating and hyperbole. Review your document to remove words ending in "y," such as "very" and "extremely," that can overstate your case. Also avoid the use of "all," "every," and "always," for the same reason. Keep your statements simple and direct and supported with evidence. Hyperbole (deliberate exaggeration) achieves the opposite effect than intended because it tends to be received skeptically by readers. For example, statements like, "our customers are our only priority," "customer service is our most important job," or "our most treasured asset is our customer" are viewed by customers as overstatements, and customers often react negatively.

CHAPTER 8

LEGAL CONSIDERATIONS IN PROPOSALS

A s you consider the writing and presentation of your proposal, you should be aware of legal considerations that need to be addressed.

Pre-Qualifying Clients

In any business, there is a need to verify that the person who is interested in your products or services has the money to pay you and will treat you ethically and equitably. Most businesses pre-qualify customers in some way. In retail, the qualification process usually takes place at the time of sale, when the customer presents a credit card, check, or cash. Sometimes the qualification can fail, as in the case of a check that is no good because of non-sufficient funds (NSF), or a declined credit card. Since the amounts involved are typically small, this is not a huge problem.

Presenting a business proposal that involves thousands of dollars requires a higher level of pre-qualification of your customer. It is not safe to assume that because a company has been in business for many years they pay their bills on time. Many companies operate close to the edge in cash flow, and they may not be as able to pay as you think. It is better to check the credit of your potential clients than it is to assume they are trustworthy and discover later they are not.

There are several things you can and should do to pre-qualify a client before you begin work:

- You can check the Dun and Bradstreet (D&B rating) at **www.dnb.com** for larger companies. For a small amount, you can order a credit report to find out the credit rating of the company, so you can tell if they pay their bills on time.

- You can request a credit report for an individual or a company. The three large credit reporting agencies (Equifax, Experian, and TransUnion) can assist you with obtaining credit reports on clients — both companies and individuals.

- You can check the Better Business Bureau at **www.bbb.com** to determine if there are any complaints by customers against the company.

In some cases, you may need to have a release signed by the company or the individual to allow you to check credit. If the clients do not want to sign the release, this may tell you something about their credit.

Non-Disclosure Agreements

Consider adding a non-disclosure agreement to your proposal, depending on the type of client and the product or service you are presenting. A non-disclosure agreement (NDA), sometimes called a confidentiality agreement, is a legal document that describes the confidential material presented to the client and the restrictions on the disclosure of the information by the client. Along with the discussion of the restrictions, penalties for disclosure are outlined.

Usually, an NDA is requested before the formal business proposal is presented to a client, so that both parties understand the information being presented is confidential or proprietary in nature, and disclosure of that information would damage the company doing the presentation. Believe it or not, there are some companies and individuals who request business proposals to obtain confidential information, so having all potential clients sign an NDA before you show them your proposal is a good precaution to take.

The NDA document will include:

- A description of the confidential information, including patents, trademarks and service marks, knowledge, financial information, business strategies, drawings and designs, and, in some cases, the language of the proposal itself.

- Information that is excluded from the restrictions, including:

  o Information the client knew already from other sources

  o Information you already discussed with the client

  o Materials generally available to the public

  o Information or materials that may be subject to subpoena for another purpose

- The term of the agreement

- Agreement on penalties for violation, including your ability to place the client under injunction to stop the continued violation. This section may also include a monetary value for the information, to provide a guideline for further fines and penalties.

This NDA sounds serious, and you may think the information you possess is not important, but consider this scenario: You present a proposal on a new office system you have developed. The clients say they are not interested, but immediately take the information and use their business contacts to sell it to others. You have now been cut out of the market and have no recourse except to get a court order to make them stop selling your system.

Thinking about these legal considerations will help you prevent costly mistakes in your business proposal and in the work you are doing with clients.

CHAPTER 9

USING DEFINITION AND
DESCRIPTION IN PROPOSALS

Before you begin writing your business proposal, stop and review all of the key terms and concepts you must convey to your reader. Determine which of these concepts and terms you must explain further to gain your audience's understanding of the subject of the proposal. Develop a list of the terms and concepts for which you will need to write a more complete definition or description.

Writing Definitions

When you have developed a list of terms that require more complete explanation, you may want to use a definition to describe some of these terms. At its most basic, a definition has a specific format which includes:

A. The term being defined

B. The class or group to which the term belongs

C. The characteristics which distinguish this term from others in the same category

As you write definitions, keep in mind the following suggestions:

- Be sure you stay within the format provided above. Avoid expressions such as, "A microwave is when you . . . " or "Schizophrenia is where someone . . . "

- Avoid circular definitions, like "A full-time employee is one who works full time," or, less obvious but still circular, "A full-time employee is one who works more than part time."

If you use all three elements — term being defined, class to which the term belongs, and distinguishing characteristics — you will be able to construct meaningful and accurate definitions of the terms you are using in your business proposal.

In many cases, a simple definition of a term or expression is not enough, and you will need to expand the definition. There are three levels of definitions, based on how much is included in the definition. Here are the three levels of definitions:

Level One

A level one definition is inserted into the sentence. Often these insertions are in the form of a parenthetical expression (inserted into the sentence within parentheses, like this one). Here are some examples:

A catalyst, an element which aids in a chemical reaction, can be . . .

We are confident that this extemporaneous (without preparation) presentation will . . .

It is likely the oil companies in this country will be nationalized (taken over by the government).

Distilled (purified) water will be used in all instances . . .

Level Two

A level two definition is included in the text in a separate sentence following the term. These insertions are often parenthetical also. Here are some examples:

> *The presentation is based on common principles of macroeconomic theory. Macroeconomic theory is an economic theory which looks at the larger areas of concern, such as countries, industries, and global trends.*

> *An analysis shows the break-even point at $480,000 in sales. The break-even point was calculated as: Fixed costs + [1- variable costs as percent of total sales].*

> *Your FICO score is a representation of the level of your creditworthiness. FICO scores range from 0 to over 800, and a score of 650 or better is considered excellent by lenders.*

Level Three

A level three definition expands the simple definition in some way to provide the reader with a more complete understanding of the concept. Depending upon your audience, you may decide to expand a definition in one or more ways:

- **Exemplification.** Through examples and analogy. Most common exemplification is provided within the body of a paragraph. Here is an example of exemplification:

> *Breakeven analysis is a key method of analysis in small businesses, particularly those with product sales. This analysis separates fixed and variable costs, and using the calculation: Fixed costs + [1- variable costs as percent of total sales]. For example, a manufacturer whose sales were $750,000, and whose fixed costs were $250,000 a month and whose variable costs were 55 percent of sales would have a break-even point of $587,500 a month.*

- **Comparison/contrast.** It is often helpful when describing something to compare it to or contrast it with something familiar. This form of expanded definition is helpful when the term being defined is complex, and your audience would have difficulty understanding it, or when it is difficult to describe in words. If you know, for example, that your reader has a limited understanding of what a rugby ball is, you could compare it to a soccer ball by describing similarities, and then contrast it with the soccer ball by explaining differences.

- **Illustration.** In some cases, it may be necessary to include an illustration, photo, or drawing of the term being described, rather than using a verbal definition. In these cases, the verbal definition or description is inadequate to explain the term. For example, if you were discussing a medieval cathedral, you may need to provide an illustration of several of its features, including a gargoyle or a flying buttress. In other cases, a simple diagram, chart, or table can be inserted into the text or provided in a separate box to more fully provide the reader with an understanding of the subject.

- **Etymology** (word origin). Often, providing the origin of a word or term gives the reader a better understanding of the use of a word in your proposal. This method of exemplification is helpful to readers with a medium to high level of education, because they need to understand basic principles of word origins to grasp what you are doing. For example, the definition of the term "cognitive dissonance" can be broken down into its roots and re-assembled for enhanced meaning. Cognitive comes from the root "cognos," meaning, "To know or to recognize." Dissonance can be divided into "Dis-" meaning "bad" and "sona" meaning "sound." So the word "cognitive dissonance" can be read as "recognizing a bad sound."

- **Operational.** An operational definition provides more meaning by explaining how something works or by describing the process by which it operates. To define the term "photosynthesis," for example, you may want to provide a brief explanation of how photosynthesis operates:

  In the process of photosynthesis, living organisms convert light energy into chemical energy. Specifically, carbon dioxide and water use sunlight to create oxygen and carbohydrates.

If you have written an extended definition in a business proposal, there are different ways you can insert that definition into the body of the proposal:

1. You can insert the extended definition in a separate paragraph, box, or section within the body of the report, in the same area where the original term was presented.

2. You can place the extended definitions in a separate section of the report or at the end in an appendix.

It is best to include the extended definition as near as possible to the term being defined so your reader has the opportunity to review the extended definition in the context of the specific section of the report. In other cases, if the insertion of definitions would break the flow of the narrative or there are too many to insert into one section, you may decide to insert definitions in a separate section.

If you decide to provide definitions in a separate section later in the proposal, be sure to alert your reader to the presence of these definitions so the reader can refer to that section. You can write this notice within a sentence, or you can create a box in which you inform the reader of the existence of the definition section. In an online proposal, or one that is being read online, you could include an internal link to the definition section.

To create an internal link within a business proposal in Microsoft Word:

1. Go to the beginning of the definition.

2. Click on the Insert menu and then "Bookmark."

3. Create a unique name for the Bookmark.

4. Go to the place where you want the link, highlight the text to be linked, and click "Insert" then "Hyperlink" (or you can click the Hyperlink Icon in the standard toolbar).

5. Click the area titled "Bookmark" in the dialog box.

6. Click the specific bookmark.

7. A link to that bookmark will be created.

Matching Definitions to Specific Audiences

Matching definition method to the characteristics and technical level of your audience can help you create an understanding of your product or service, and can help you forge better relationships with your audience. At all levels of knowledge, it is a good idea to include at least one example for your definition. Sometimes you can include the example in the sentence where you create the definition. If this is not possible, insert the example directly after the definition.

Low Technical Knowledge. For an audience with little technical knowledge, use operational definitions to provide more explanation. Be careful not to include technical terms in your definition that need further explanation. In the definition of photosynthesis above, for example, you might want to take out the word "carbohydrates" and replace it with "sugars and starches" to be clear. Audiences with little technical knowledge also appreciate illustrations and other graphics to aid understanding.

Some Technical Knowledge. If your audience has an advanced degree of knowledge about your subject, you may be able to use shorter definitions, comparisons and contrasts, and illustrations. You may also be able to define terms by using more technical terms that are familiar to your audience.

High Technical Knowledge. If your audience has an advanced level of technical knowledge about your proposal, you can use even more technical terms in your definition, and you can define new terms in light of familiar technical terms. In addition, you may want to include etymology for your term, which may be of interest to this audience, and could help them understand your definition.

CHAPTER 10

USING CREATIVITY TECHNIQUES
TO PLAN YOUR PROPOSAL

Most people who begin preparing a business proposal think in terms of structure, outline, and analysis. But there is another possibility you may find useful in thinking about your business proposal: using right-brain function to plan more creatively. While it is not a good idea to generalize about brain function, there is a belief that the two hemispheres of the brain (right and left) differ in their functioning. The left brain is said to function in a manner that is more sequential, analytical, verbal, and logical; the right brain is said to be more holistic, imagistic, and intuitive in its functions.

There are a number of possible ways to include creativity and intuition in the process of preparing a business proposal. Some of the more common creative processes are listed and described in this section.

Six Hats Thinking. The "six hats" thinking model was created by psychologist Edward de Bono to describe various ways in which a problem could be addressed and solved. Each of the hats represents a way the thinking process could be conducted. The six hats method helps encourage creative thinking, and is said to improve communication and speed up the decision process. The six hats are:

- **White Hat.** The white hat is characterized by a blank sheet and is the objective way of thinking, relying on information, reports, facts, and figures.

- **Red Hat.** The red hat, characterized by fire, represents intuition, opinion, and emotion in thinking and decision making.

- **Yellow Hat.** The yellow hat, characterized by the sun, represents positive thinking and praise; yellow-hat thinking states why it will work.

- **Black Hat.** The black hat, characterized by a judge's robes, represents criticism, judgment, and negative (why it will not work) thinking.

- **Green Hat.** The green hat, characterized by a plant, represents new approaches and alternatives, generation of new ideas, and an "everything goes" attitude toward the problem.

- **Blue Hat.** The blue hat, characterized by the sky, represents "big picture" thinking, overview, and overall processes; the blue hat is a "meta" hat.

Using all of the hats in a discussion helps the group come to a better solution to a problem or a more thorough discussion of the issues. For example, if your company is preparing a proposal and you want to be certain that you have thought of every possibility — positive and negative — you could gather a group of individuals and have each assume the position of one hat. Carrying on a discussion between the "hats" can bring many viewpoints to the problem. In the case of the discussion of whether or not to prepare a proposal:

- White hat presents the facts.

- Red hat presents the emotional element.

- Black hat is critical and negative ("it is not a good idea").

- Yellow hat is positive ("this is a great idea").

- Green hat is creative and has lots of ideas.

- Blue hat controls the process and keeps the group thinking about the "big picture."

Brainstorming. This problem-solving technique developed in the 1930s, is used in groups to generate many creative ideas. Although it has been argued that traditional brainstorming does not increase the effectiveness of a group or its output, it may be used as a team-building exercise in a situation where many people in a company must work together to produce a business proposal.

The principles behind brainstorming are intended to reduce inhibitions and encourage idea generation. These principles are:

1. **Focus on quantity.** Individuals in the group are encouraged to come up with ideas, no matter how silly or useless they may seem. From the large quantity of ideas, some will emerge as more useful, and these may be selected later for further consideration.

2. **No criticism.** This principle involves suspension of judgment. During a brainstorming exercise, many ideas may be generated. To encourage quantity, no one is allowed to comment.

3. **Combine and improve ideas.** After the initial brainstorming session in which ideas are encouraged and criticism is not allowed, the group reviews all ideas, culling out those that are not workable, and combining similar ideas into new and improved ones.

This synergistic interaction can produce a wealth of excellent ideas, which can be used in the generation of a stronger business proposal. The additional benefits of this creative exercise are building loyalty to the idea in the individuals who participated, and creating a stronger team mindset as the proposal moves forward.

Use brainstorming to try to figure out what the client wants. Ask your group to "think like the client" and ask people to come up with ideas for what you can do to prepare a business proposal that addresses the client's concerns and satisfies the client's needs.

Mind Mapping. A mind map, according to Wikipedia, is "a diagram used to represent words, ideas, tasks or other items linked to and arranged in a radius around a central key word or idea." A mind map is useful in generating ideas within a structure, and in seeing the relationship between concepts within the structure. Mind maps have been used as aids in problem solving and organization.

While mind maps can be used by individuals in note-taking. They are also a good device for brainstorming, because they create an easy-to-see diagram that shows inter-relationships. Mind maps can be drawn by hand or with the use of computer software, and they are best used by individuals or small groups.

To create a mind map, begin in the middle with a central word, phrase, or idea, and branch out with keywords and concepts. You may want to use colors, images, and symbols to assist you and your group in the creation of the mind map. Draw lines connecting each concept to others and back to the central image, from which everything flows. Use a mind map to create an overview of your proposal, and use this mind map to create an outline or table of contents for the business proposal.

Storyboarding. A storyboard is an organized way to describe a process or tell a story. Storyboarding was first used at Walt Disney's studios in the 1930s, and it was adapted to business use. Today, many companies use storyboarding concepts in a variety of ways to plan advertising and promotion campaigns and to prepare business proposals. More recently, storyboarding is used in Web development to create a graphic representation of a Web site. Using a storyboard allows a developer or planner to experiment easily, making changes on the storyboard in a proposal or online before they are finalized. The visual element allows a group of people to view the board and make changes, re-arranging the sections and order to create new possibilities.

These techniques are presented to encourage you and your company to use alternative ways of thinking about the problems and issues related to a business proposal. As you think about the proposal, you may want to do some "six hats" thinking about whether you want to take on this project. Or you may want to get a group together to brainstorm possible solutions to the client's problem before you begin to put the proposal on paper. If you are working alone in creating your business proposal, you may want to spend some time creating a mind map to help you think about the structure and relationships inherent in your proposal.

There are many applications for these creative techniques, and they may prove helpful if you are stuck on a problem and you need a creative nudge in a new direction. In addition, these techniques may be helpful at different points in the process. For example, brainstorming at the beginning of a project can save you from going down a path that may not work. In the same way, preparing a storyboard can help you lay out the path of a complex proposal. If you are stuck in the middle of proposal writing, stop and think about creating a mind map. In any case, do not discount the value of right-brain approaches to business proposal writing.

What to do with the results of your creative thinking:

1. Prioritize.

2. Put it directly into your proposal. For example, a version of your storyboard could go into the proposal to show the timeline and process you will use to satisfy the client's needs.

3. Turn a mind map into an outline for your business proposal.

CHAPTER 11

GATHERING DATA FOR YOUR PROPOSAL

Your proposal will be improved by the addition of external data. Not only does this information add to your credibility, but it gives additional emphasis to your points. Social authority is a powerful persuader, so using data and quotes from authorities and specialists will help you make your case.

Some of the information you find in doing research for your business proposal may be included in the final report, and some may be for your own use. For example, information on competitors may be helpful to you so you can create a USP (unique selling proposition), but you may not want to share this information in the report. If you were creating a startup business plan, on the other hand, you may want to list all of your direct competitors to show that you understand your position in the market.

Sources of Data

Use data in your business proposal to support your points. This data can include dates, results from experiments, demographics, government reports and statistics, and information from journals in your field.

Internet Sources. Data may often come from the Internet. For example, if you are writing a proposal about productivity, you could go to the Bureau of Labor Statistics (**www.bls.gov**) to find productivity data by business subsector. If you were discussing your competitive advantage in your areas of specialization, you may want to use the Thomas Register (**www. thomasnet.com**) to find all of the competitors in your field or in your geographical area.

Interviews. Interviews with authorities and experts are another good source of information to include in your business proposal. Here are some suggestions for making these interactions more productive:

- Call or e-mail the individual and request an interview. Explain in detail the purpose for your request and ask for a specific, short amount of time (no more than an hour). This will allow her to determine how much time will be needed, and it will make her decision of whether or not to be interviewed easier. Send your prepared list of questions ahead of time so the interviewee has time to read and think about them. Some interviewees prefer to answer your questions before the interview; this gives you time to expand on questions and ask more detailed and interesting questions that may develop during the interview.

- Prepare for the interview by learning as much as possible about the individual. Check out his Web site; read his books and articles, particularly the most recent ones. In other words, do your homework.

- Prepare a list of possible questions that relate to the subject you want to discuss. Start with some general background questions and move on to more specific questions. After you have selected the general background questions, list the questions in order of importance, with the most important questions first. Some interviewees can answer a question in a few words, while others take a great deal of time and provide lengthy explanations for each question. If you list the questions in order of importance, you will be sure to get your most important questions answered. Prepare more questions than you think you will need, so that you have enough questions for the person who answers each question only briefly.

- Use a tape recorder so you do not have to rely on memory or notes. You may still want to take notes, but you will have the recording as backup. Be sure to ask the interviewee if it is all right to use the recorder; if the person says "no," turn off the recorder.

- Stop the interview at the agreed-upon time, so as to honor your commitment to stay within the time frame. Only extend the interview beyond this time if the interviewee gives permission.

- After the interview, write up your notes and prepare a summary and a short biographical sketch of the individual. Send the summary and biography to the interviewee for approval. Depending upon how you are using the material in your business plan, you may also want to have the person approve the final copy.

- When you write the results of the interview, stick to exact quotes and paraphrase accurately. Do not embellish or add to answers. Use only the material given; do not get too creative.

Case Studies. Another good source of information for your business proposal is a case study. Case studies involve in-depth examination of a single instance or event. They can provide evidence for your business proposal in the same way as a testimonial or a reference. Case studies can also give prospective clients a visual representation of how others have benefited from your products or services. Several forms of case studies may be useful to you in your proposal:

- **Critical instance case studies** provide evidence of how another institution solved a critical problem. Using such a case study, particularly if it involves use of your company's products or services, can be helpful in creating a sense of urgency in your client.

- **Program effectiveness case studies** describe how a client implemented a program and the results of that program on productivity or other outcomes.

- **Narrative case studies** are used to tell a story about another company or individual who used products or services similar to yours to solve a problem.

Research Results. You may have done research in your field of study, or you may have results of research done by others that you can include in your business proposal. Research results can be used to support your proposal and to provide clients with assurance about the viability of your approach to the problem. For example, if you are a mental health professional presenting a proposal to a corporation on the effects of counseling on employee productivity, research from other companies can be effective in making your case.

Survey Results. Surveys are a good way to present data to show satisfaction with a product or service, or to show acceptance and approval. You can create your own survey using an online tool such as Survey Monkey (**www. surveymonkey.com**), by mailing out a survey to past clients, or by hiring a survey company to conduct the survey for you.

Analyze Your Data Sources

Before including specific data in your business proposal, be sure it comes from a reputable source. The most effective data is recent, valid, reliable, unbiased, useful, and as close to the primary source as possible. If you include data in your proposal that does not meet these benchmarks, you may undermine or even destroy the effectiveness of your presentation.

Consider the following principles of data integrity in more detail:

- **Recent.** The knowledge base in any field changes rapidly. What was known to be true a few years ago may now be disproved. The more recent the data, the more likely it is to be positively received.

- **Valid.** Validity in research addresses the question of whether the researcher is measuring what she says is being measured. A study is valid if it measures what is supposed to be measured. The concept of validity also includes logic — the results must logically follow from the research or the thought process. For example, if you said, "All dogs are smart. Men are smart. Therefore, men are dogs," your argument would not be logical. Validity also includes the issue of cause and effect; just because one thing follows another in time does not mean the second is the cause of the first. When using statistics, make sure they make sense to you before you use them in a proposal.

- **Reliable.** Reliability is another important characteristic of good data. Data is reliable if it measures the same way consistently. Another way to look at reliability is to say that the data is able to be replicated; if the same test was done in different circumstances, it would yield the same results. In the social sciences in particular, it is important that data be reliable, since the subjects are humans, who are infinitely variable. For example, one study that indicated a high correlation between performance on a test and eating chocolate before the test must be performed many times to be certain that it is reliable and not just a one-time result.

- **Unbiased.** Reliability also relates to sources — the source of your data must be reliable. If you are citing an authority, that person must be acknowledged as an expert, and the person's expertise must relate to the subject area under discussion. An expert in one area is not necessarily an expert in another. In addition, the person or source must not be seen as having a conflict of interest; for example, the person should not be promoting a product or service which she sells or receives profits from.

The Internet is a particularly obvious realm of biased information. Before you cite an online source in a business proposal, check carefully the background of the individual or company. One good way to do this is to read the "About Us" page of the Web site; look at the credentials of the principal individuals in the organization. Also, check to see if the Web site is selling or promoting anything. Some sites appear to be unbiased, but they may actually be advocating a cause. For example, some organizations oppose vaccinations; they may have anti-vaccination material on their site that supposedly is unbiased, but is actually produced to show the negative effects of vaccinations.

- **Primary.** Always attempt to find primary data over secondary data. Primary data is direct, raw, unprocessed data. Information from government agencies is, for the most part, primary data. For example, census data is presented in readable form, but no attempt has been made to analyze this information. In science, primary data would be the computer printout of a test; in history, it may be the letters of a famous person. Because it has not undergone any intervention or analysis, primary data is the most reliable form of data.

Compiling and Including Data

After you have collected the data you will be using in your business proposal, you will need to decide how to present this information. Here are some suggestions for presentation of data:

- **Internal Citations.** You can present data within the context of the report itself. That is, you incorporate the data into the narrative within the sentences and paragraphs. Internal citations are the simplest way to include less complex data. For example, if you want to include information on the Consumer Price Index from the Bureau of Labor Statistics, you might state:

> According to the Bureau of Labor Statistics (2007), the Consumer Price Index (CPI) rose 0.8 percent in November 2007; since November 2006, the CPI has risen 4.3 percent.

Internal citations are also appropriate for quotes from interviews and for summary results from surveys and research.

- **Embedded Graphics.** For more complex data or data that lends itself to graphical form, you can insert the graphic into the text at the appropriate point. The graphics section in Chapter 19 is one example of embedding graphics into text. The easiest way to insert graphics in this manner is to "cut" the graphics from one application or from the Internet, and "paste" the graphic into the text. You may need to re-size the graphic before or after inserting it.

- **Embedded Text Boxes.** To provide interest on a page, and to make your data stand out, you may want to include it as a text box within a page. For example, some of the interviews in this book are included as text boxes. This may be a good technique for critical case studies or interviews that are important to your proposal. To create a text box, simply use the "Outside Border" feature of Microsoft Word to surround the text.

- **Appendixes.** For some types of complex or detailed data, it may be best to refer briefly to the information in the body of the proposal and include the full citation in narrative or table form as an appendix. If you are using an appendix, you will need to refer the reader to this information. For example, you may write:

The Bureau of Labor Statistics has further information about employment rates and changes in unemployment rates over the past five years. See Appendix B for this information.

Giving Credit to Sources

Whenever you include sources in your business proposal, you must adhere to certain protocols in presentation and citation. In other words, you must provide information about your sources to avoid plagiarism and so your client can find further information about this subject. The principle of citation requires that you provide enough information so the reader can be directed to the bibliography at the end of your proposal. In most cases, this means including the author and date of the work. For example, if you were citing the Bureau of Labor Statistics information, you would need to insert "Bureau of Labor Statistics, 2007" along with the text being quoted. Note the example above. If you have two citations from the same author in the same year, you will need to add more information in order to distinguish them. For example, if you have two citations from the Bureau of Labor Statistic in 2007, you may need to include a few words from the title in your citation.

Citation Style Guides. There are several recognized style guides and protocols that researchers and authors of scholarly publications use to cite sources and prepare bibliographies or lists of works cited; the style you use depends upon the type of publication.

- For works in the humanities, language, and historical areas, Modern Language Association (MLA) standards are used.

- For works in the social sciences, like psychology and sociology, the American Psychological Association (APA) style is used.

- For works in research, Vancouver or Chicago style is used.

If you are creating a general business proposal, you can probably use any style you wish, as long as you are consistent within your work. Many business publications use APA style, so you may want to use this one.

> The important thing to remember is that you must cite your sources; that is, information on the source of your information, so you can tell your reader that you are not claiming someone else's work as your own.

Embedded Citations. If you are citing sources within the body of the proposal, you can cite your source in one of two ways:

- Within the sentence, as in the example above, for the Bureau of Labor Statistics. The words, "according to" are acceptable, along with the date in parentheses.

- In parentheses at the end of the sentence. In the example above, this citation may look like this:

> The Consumer Price Index (CPI) rose 0.8 percent in November 2007; since November 2006, the CPI has risen 4.3 percent (Bureau of Labor Statistics, 2007).

Embedded Graphics and Text Boxes. If you are including a graphic within the text or a text box, include the same type of citation directly under the graphic. A citation for an embedded graphic may look like this:

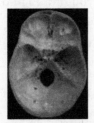

(Source: **http://en.wikipedia.org/w/index.php?title=Foramen&oldid=142641874**)

Footnotes and Endnotes. In recent years, use of footnotes has diminished. Most writers include citations within the text. You can include a footnote in Microsoft Word by clicking on "Insert," then, "Reference," then, "Footnote," and then typing the text. The application automatically numbers the footnotes and adjusts page lengths to include the footnotes. Endnotes are sometimes included, using the same process as for footnotes above, and selecting the "Endnote" option.

Creating a Reference List

If you cite sources within your business proposal, you will need to create a bibliography, works cited list, or reference list in addition to citing your sources in the text or as footnotes or endnotes. To help you decide which to use, here is an explanation of each of these option:

- **Bibliography.** A bibliography is a listing of works to which the reader can refer for more information on the subject. The works which you have cited in the text are also included in this bibliography.

- **Works Cited.** A works cited list includes only references cited in the text.

- **References.** A reference list is the same as a works cited list, including only references cited in the text.

To present references in one of these lists, include all of your sources in alphabetical order by author. As with the internal citations, you should find a reference protocol that fits the style of proposal you are writing and use that for all of your citations.

Citing Sources in Your Proposal

There are many styles you can use for citing sources within the text of your proposal. Here are some examples of citations in APA format (all examples are fictitious):

Book: Smith, R. (2001). *Management Theories*. New York, NY: Standard Press.

Periodical: Smith, E. (2005). The use of citations in business proposals. *Journal of Proposals,* 14, 253–263. (Note that the first number is the Volume (14), and the second set of numbers are pages (253–263).

Newspaper article: Smith, M. (2003, September 16). *Business proposals: New formats for success.* The Jonestown News-Gazette, pp. 1, 8.

Internet source: Smith, A.A. (2005). "Business Proposal Formats." Retrieved: October 3, 2007 from **www.aasmith.com/proposalformats**.

Note that if you print out the page for the Internet source, you can find the date it was retrieved on the bottom of the page, along with the URL (Web address).

Interview (unpublished): N. Smith, personal communication. Smith, Nebraska. October 11, 2003.

Note that all you need to include for an interview is the name of the person being interviewed, and the date and place of the interview.

Film or videotape: Jones, P. B. (Producer), & Hart, B. a. (Director). (2002). *Creating Effective Business Proposals* [DVD]. New York, NY: AgentAFilms.

CASE STUDY: MEGAN MURRAY

Acquisitions Officer

Megan Murray has been with a large international insurance company since 2001, and she has been an acquisitions officer since 2006. In her present position, she prepares and review many different types of proposals. In November 2006, she prepared and presented a white paper on the emerging subject of

CASE STUDY: MEGAN MURRAY

"green" building, to a management conference. See Chapter 23 for a discussion of white papers as proposals.

The white paper began as an unsolicited proposal, as Megan originally intended the paper to be informational for her own use and for other asset managers. After she began her work, she discovered that the subject of "green building" was on the agenda at the management conference, so she offered to provide this information to the attendees.

She began her research on the subject from reading the many journals and publications in the real estate industry, pulling information from articles and sections on "green" products, "green" buildings, "green" real estate, and about Leadership in Energy and Environmental Design (LEED) certification for individuals in the building and design trades. She found most of her information on the Internet, particularly from other papers and from the USGBC (U.S. Green Building Council), a nonprofit organization dedicated to "sustainable business practices" (**www. usgbc.org**).

Megan was careful to cite sources correctly by providing Web site URLs and other appropriate citations. Graphs and charts were titled and sources were cited for each. She found several professionals who discussed how they incorporated environmentally responsible products and systems into building, and she included their comments, also being careful to give them credit. Her fifteen-page paper included eight sources.

Because she had only a limited time to finish the paper in time for the conference, Megan regrets not having enough time for more interviews. If she had it to do over, she would have done more research before doing interviews, so she would have been able to ask more informed questions.

As a result of Megan's white paper, the company formed a new "Green Team" (which Megan heads) to create a mission statement and determine how the company will integrate this new trend into current real estate functions.

She has some suggestions for others working on a white paper of this type:

- Begin by discussing terminology, and explaining the basics.

- Read everything you can for background; you may not use it all, but it will all be helpful in the overall proposal.

CASE STUDY: MEGAN MURRAY

- Do your background research before doing interviews so you can carefully plan your questions.

- Check the backgrounds and biases of your interviewees. Know where they stand on the issues.

- Check and double check; proofread and have others critique and proofread your paper.

- Most important, consider your audience and its needs. Do not overwhelm your readers with all of the details. Most readers just want the basics, so do not give them an in-depth presentation. Give them the highlights and let them read the proposal later.

CHAPTER 12

Costing a Proposal

Your business proposal will need to include information on costs and pricing. Preparing an accurate and complete cost estimate is the single most important part of the proposal. Your cost estimate must be accurate so that both you and the client can rely on the costs for discussion and implementation of the proposal; and it must be complete, including specific costs for all resources utilized in the project.

Resource-Based Costing

Costs are based on resources — time, materials, people, and overhead (facilities, utilities, maintenance). Resources translate into monetary costs. For example:

- **Time.** If you are preparing a proposal for your time as a professional, you will need to be certain that you have placed enough value on your time to receive an adequate compensation for your work. Some clients may want to see a total cost for your time on the project, but you may want to break down the cost into hourly time. For example, if you are a graphic artist doing an illustration for a book, your client may want you to estimate the cost for the illustration. A portion of that cost is for your time, but another element is your creativity, which cannot be measured. The creativity cost may have to be built into your time.

- **Materials.** You will also need to estimate material costs for the project, including office supplies, and specific materials needed to complete the work. This estimate should be relatively easy, since you can obtain cost lists for materials.

- **People.** If you have employee or subcontractors working with you on a project, you will need to estimate their time and charges. For employees, you can use an hourly rate (including the cost of any benefits they may receive from you), or a charge rate, which is higher. In government contracting jobs, for example, you can use a charge rate, which is the amount you charge to the project for each hour of work time. You may pay an engineer $35 an hour plus benefits, but bill out this person's time at $75 an hour for the project. Time for other professionals such as attorneys and accountants is charged in the same manner.

- **Overhead.** Depending upon the type of project, you may want to include overhead charges in your cost estimate. These costs would include a proportion of rent or mortgage payments, utilities, phone, maintenance, and other charges which are part of doing business. If the people working on your project are using your office facilities, the cost of your project should reflect these charges.

Effective Costing Strategies

Finding the "right" cost for a project is tricky, because costing too low can result in working on a project for little or no profit, while costing too high can result in no project at all. Before you begin to work on project costs as you are preparing your business proposal, go to the section on Creating a Value Statement in Chapter 6 and read the Success Story in Chapter 26.

Think about how you can present your project costs through the lens of this value statement. Here are some other questions to get you started on determining how to cost a proposal, keeping client needs in mind:

- **What is my client's financial situation?** How has the client presented his expectation of price? Some clients will begin the cost conversation by stating, "Money is no object." This may or may not be true; the client may be stating that he wants you to cost the project to the best of your ability so he can see the highest possible cost. Other clients may start out with a fixed budget and require that you adhere to this amount. In this case, you may have to decide that you might not be able to effectively cost the project to give you what you want.

- **What is my "rock bottom" price?** You can find your "rock bottom" price by using the resource-based costing approach described above or through another method for determining costs. Determine a cost number that you cannot lower under any circumstances; this number would not include any profit, but would merely be enough to cover costs. For example, your rock bottom cost may include amounts you must pay employees or subcontractors, and amounts you must pay for travel expenses to work on the project. Another way to look at "rock bottom" cost is that it must include costs you cannot recover from the project. This number is your "rock bottom" cost, and you will need to know this number as you go into price negotiations (described below).

- **What will this project gain me?** The "gain", in most cases, will be expressed as a profit for you and your company. In other words, any price estimate above "rock bottom" would include some profit for you and your company. In some cases, your "gain" may be intangible, and may include the possibilities of greater media exposure from this project, the prospect of a valued testimonial from the client, or your ability to use this project as a stepping-stone to other projects. If you are new to this field, winning a high-exposure project, which can be useful to promoting your career, maybe enough of a gain to allow you to take a project that just provides "rock bottom" return.

Use all three of these questions to help you in the price negotiations you will be involved in when you present your proposal.

Negotiating Price

If you are skillful in presenting your price estimates, you may not be required to undertake a negotiation of these prices. Presenting your price as "non-negotiable" may be appropriate in some situations, while in other situations your first price will be considered a "take-off" point for negotiation between you and the client. If you need to negotiate your price, here are some tips that may help you gain the best possible price, while still maintaining a good relationship with the client:

- **Do your research.** If you have thoroughly prepared for your proposal presentation, you may already have all the information you need on this client. If not, you will need to find out about the client's financial situation and how this person or company negotiates. Talk with other vendors in other areas to see what their experiences have been with this client. Talk to employees to see what they know about the chief negotiator's style. Go into the negotiation with as much information as possible.

- **Present your value statement early in the discussion.** If you can establish a high value for your proposal in the mind of the client, you are in a much better position to negotiate for a high price. Provide the client with as much information as possible about how this proposal can save time or money, increase productivity or decrease attrition — whatever is appropriate in the situation.

- **Never make the first move.** It is likely that you will be required to present your price in the proposal, but if you think you may have to negotiate, let the buyer make the first offer. This strategy is important in all kinds of negotiation situations, including salary offers. If you present the first number, you are locked in; you cannot go too much higher, and you may be forced to go lower. If you can wait out the other person and force her to present an expected cost, you are in a better position. One way to do this is to ask, "What would you be wiling to pay to receive this valuable product or service that can save you $300,000 over the next year?"

- **Never look too eager.** People can sense when you want something badly; this gives them a tool to use against you in the negotiations. For example, if you are buying a house, do not let the real estate agent see that you desperately want a house. Give the impression that you are not impressed.

- **Be willing to walk away.** If you have your "rock bottom" price firmly set and you know what your gain is, you may need to walk away from the project if the client wants you to go below this amount. Accept the fact that you cannot win every deal, and that some projects are not worth your time and money. In some cases, your willingness to walk away may result in your getting the project at an acceptable price; if not, you can spend your time looking for more profitable projects.

- **Assume the client needs you.** The client would not be talking about prices if he had not already made the decision to hire you for this project. If you are talking about prices, the deal is almost done; you just have to agree on price. Unless the client is totally unreasonable about price, you probably have the project. So sit back and hold fast to your predetermined bottom limits.

- **Keep silent; listen and learn.** In most cases, the person who talks first loses most. Use the strategy often employed by police officers; they sit silently waiting for the other person to speak. Most people cannot handle silence, so they are forced to start talking. Their talk reveals information about them that you can use. The less you talk, the better your position in the negotiations.

- **Stay calm and polite.** Never raise your voice or get angry. Do not take anything personally in the negotiation; remember, it is just business. Getting angry may lose you the project; it certainly will raise doubts in the mind of the client.

- **Everything is negotiable; think trade-offs.** This is the reason you have a "rock bottom" price. If the client will not accept your price, consider what you can trade-off to get a higher price. There may be elements you can leave out of the project, or the client may decide to lengthen the timeline.

- **Always have a BATNA.** The term "BATNA" stands for "best alternative to a negotiated agreement." In other words, the BATNA is your fall-back position if the price negotiations do not succeed. In some cases, your BATNA may be to walk away from the project; in other cases, it may be for you to change the scope or details of the agreement. Before you begin to discuss price with your client, be sure you have determined your BATNA — what you will do if the negotiations break down.

CHAPTER 13

DESIGNING AND FORMATTING YOUR BUSINESS PROPOSAL

Acceptance of your business proposal depends on your ability to write an effective document, but presentation is also important. As you plan your proposal, you may want to include the services of advisors who are skilled in graphics and layout, and use their expertise.

Proposal Outlines

The outline of your proposal will depend to a great extent on the type of proposal, but there are some commonly accepted protocols for sections that must be included in all proposals. Here is a general outline of a business proposal:

Executive Summary. The executive summary is an important part of the proposal because it provides an overview of the entire document, and can be read quickly by those wishing to have only the "big picture" for this proposal. Typically, the executive summary is written last, after the document has been put together, but it is always placed first in the outline. See Chapter 16 for more information on preparing an executive summary for your business proposal.

Introduction and Background. This section provides the following information:

1. It states the purpose of the proposal.

2. It provides information on why the proposal is being written, including the problem or issue that gave rise to the proposal.

3. It includes information on the person or people preparing the proposal.

4. It provides information on the company or individual for whom the proposal is being written.

5. It describes your USP and value statement (both of these subjects are described in more detail in Chapter 6).

Goals and Objectives. In some short, less formal proposals, this section may be included within the introduction and background section. In formal proposals, a separate goals and objectives section is usually included. This section provides information about the goals of the proposal relating to the prospective client. For example, the goals of a proposal for a Web design project may state: "To provide a high-traffic Web site which will draw clients for the company." Because this is an important section, spend as much time as possible creating the language for this section.

Methods and Tasks. In this section, you will present the process you will use to implement the project you have described in your proposal. This is a key section because your client will want to know how you plan to create the value you described in the introduction and background section. Be sure to include a timeline for your proposal.

Conclusion. The conclusion of your proposal is important because it summarizes your value statement, the process you will use to complete the project, and the assertions you make about why the client should accept your proposal.

Proposal Document Design

One of the first tasks you will face in preparing your proposal for printing will be to determine the overall design of the document. Each element plays a part in creating a proposal that will be effective for your audience. Before you begin formatting your document, check the requirements of your prospective client. If your prospective client has created an RFP or another document setting out the requirements of the proposal, mirror that style in your proposal. For example, an RFP may contain specific required sections and proposal elements for all bidders and responders. In particular, you may need to retain the same outline form and sections as in the original document.

Here are some design element decisions you will need to make:

1. **Font Style.** There are thousands of fonts to choose from for business documents. Fonts are created in "families," or groups, of different sizes and styles such as bold, italic, and condensed. In choosing a font, consider several factors:

    a. Readability. Readability is the primary factor to consider when deciding on a font family for your business proposal. Whichever font you choose will be used throughout the proposal, so it must be one that most readers will find easily readable. For readability, use a serif font, like Times New Roman or Book Antiqua. Sans serif fonts are used primarily for headlines and design elements, and are less often used for longer documents or blocks of text. Avoid using sans serif fonts such as Arial and Tahoma, as they tend to be less readable in text-heavy documents.

    b. Style. The font you use in your proposal sets the style for your document. If you have a particular style you are attempting to portray for your company, choose a font that mirrors that style.

c. Company logo and stationery. If you have a company logo, tagline, and stationery in a specific font, you may want to use that style in all of your business proposals. If that logo is sans serif, as mentioned above, try to find a serif font that fits well with the look you want to achieve.

2. **Sentence and Paragraph Style.**

a. Double spacing between sentences was originally used to provide a clear visual break between sentences. With more modern, easy-to-read type fonts and word processing programs, it is no longer necessary to double space between sentences.

b. Most business proposals use a block format paragraph, which is a flush left style with the first line not indented and double spacing between paragraphs. This paragraph style is easy to read and easy to prepare. For some letter format proposals, though, you may want to use the semi-block style with the first line inserted five spaces and no spacing between paragraphs, to save space.

c. Use a "ragged right" style for paragraphs, unless you are using a more sophisticated software program, such as Microsoft Publisher. "Full" justification, with both right and left margins justified, is tricky to produce with most word processing software, and it results in some uneven lines. If you want to produce your proposal with full justification, Microsoft Publisher and other desktop publishing programs make the use of "full" justification easier to produce and read.

3. **Page Layout and Margins.** Use lots of white space on your pages to make your business proposal easier to read. Set the left margin at 1.5 inches, to provide room for binding and hole punching.

Set the right margin at one inch or more. Set the top margin of the first page of the proposal about a one-third of the way down the page (about 3.5 inches). The top margin for subsequent pages should be set at one inch, not including any header. This will provide adequate space between the header and the first line of the text. Set the bottom margin at one inch at a minimum; if you plan to include footnotes, set the bottom margin at 1.5 inches, so you leave some space between the footnotes and the last line of text.

4. **Widow and Orphan Controls.** The appearance of your business proposal will be improved if you set controls to prevent "widows" and "orphans." Widows are single lines left over at the end of a page, and orphans are single lines at the end of a paragraph at the top of a page. Setting controls to prevent widows and orphans will help you control the appearance of your proposal.

5. **Keep Text Together Controls.** There may be sections of text (lengthy quotations, for example), that you may want to keep together and not separate between pages. You can set your word processing application to prevent this text block from being separated.

6. **Outlining Style.** You will probably use some form of outlining within the body of your business proposal. Before you begin working, determine which outline form you want to use. The two most common possibilities for outline format are:

   a. Traditional. The traditional outline format separates levels as follows:

   Level One: Roman numerals, capitalized: I, II, III, etc.

   Level Two: English letters, uppercase: A., B., C., etc.

Level Three: Arabic numbers: 1., 2., 3., etc.

Level Four: English letters, lowercase: a., b., c., etc.

Level Five: Arabic numbers, with parentheses: 1), 2), 3), etc.

Level Six: English letters, with parentheses: a), b), c), etc.

Note that for the English letters and Arabic numbers, a period is placed after the item.

b. Section and subsection. In this format, sections within chapters are numbered, and subsections are designated as subsets of each section. This type of outline format is used most often in technical and scientific reports and proposals. Here is an example of this outline style:

Chapter 1.

Section 1.

Subsection 1.1

Subsection 1.2

Sub-subsection 1.2.1

Sub-subsection 1.2.2

Sub-sub-subsection 1.2.2.3

Consider all of these elements as you design your business proposal. The key to design is to keep all elements consistent throughout the document. For example, avoid changing font style families within the document; retain the same family throughout.

CASE STUDY: MICHELE DEFILIPPO

Owner of 1106 Design, LLC
Book Design Business
www.1106design.com
michele@1106design.com
610 East Bell Road, #2-402
Phoenix, AZ 85022-2393
602-866-3226

1106 Design delivers top-quality typography and book design to customers all over the globe. The owner, Michele DeFilippo, says the company has been in business since 1980. Michele explains that every book design project she works on begins with a detailed proposal, which offers all of the company's services. The proposal explains what is and is not included in the price. Writing the detailed proposal first requires a thorough review of the details provided by the client, with a particular eye toward identifying those areas where sufficient detail is missing. She may receive a request for a proposal that says only, "I need a book cover designed. Please send me your price list." Michele explains that she needs much more information than this to prepare an accurate proposal. She must spend time with each client to find out that person's needs and preferences.

The most impressive proposals, Michele believes, are complete and detailed. This indicates that the company is competent and experienced. She says, "I am much more likely to be impressed with a proposal that offers a detailed explanation of the services offered than one that contains only a few lines of text and a price." The most important thing for a business proposal writer to consider, she states, is to completely understand the services the client wants, and make sure your proposal addresses those client requests. Michele will often call the prospective client before submitting a proposal, just to chat. She believes that a conversation is often more revealing than a written request for a quote.

Michele works from a boilerplate document and customizes it as needed for each prospective client, adding and removing elements according to the client's requirements. Working from boilerplate documents is a cost-effective way to prepare a proposal, because most items have already been carefully proofread or edited, so it is only a matter of proofreading any new material that is added.

While speaking with the prospective client on the phone, Michele usually takes notes about client requirements. She believes it is important to take the time to write down all of the items the client requests, and to include these elements in the proposal and pricing. Each proposal must be customized to include the extra

CASE STUDY: MICHELE DEFILIPPO

time needed for these additional items. Michele says she always sticks with the price quoted, even if she has made an error and not included extra items. This is why it is important to both note the extras, and take the time to make sure they are included in the proposal and quote.

Finally, Michele suggests, "Don't put off writing the proposal until the last minute. Finish it early, and then review it a few times before it is due. If you feel yourself getting frantic and worked up, just stop, because that is surely when you will make an expensive mistake."

Proposal Formats

Before you start working on your proposal, you will need to determine the best format for this document. The type of format depends primarily on the type of proposal, how it will be presented, and to whom it will be presented.

- You may be presenting a long proposal for a major project that will occur over many months or even years, or you may be presenting a short proposal for a one-time project that will be completed quickly.

- You may be presenting a very formal proposal or an informal proposal.

- You may be presenting your business proposal to a group, or to a single individual.

- You may be presenting your proposal in person or by mail or e-mail.

- You may be presenting an internal proposal to one or more individuals, or you may be presenting an external proposal. Your proposal may be solicited or unsolicited.

Types of Formats

Before you decide on the type of format to use for your business proposal, read through this section so you can see which type might best suit the situation. Here are some of the major types of formats and the situations in which each type works best. Chapter references are included so you can see the details for each type of format.

Memo Format. Memos are written primarily to internal audiences and are usually used for more informal types of intracompany correspondence. Memos take a specific form, depending on the company; each company has its own format for memos. Memos are sometimes sent by internal company mail, but they also can be sent to multiple individuals as attachments to e-mails. A memo may have a short summary, and it may also include some of the additional elements of more formal reports, including appendixes.

Letter Format. While memos are most often informal, letters are a more formal choice of communication for business proposals. Proposals may be presented in the form of a letter for short projects that are not very complex. Letters are often used for external proposals, but may also be used for formal internal project proposals. You can use a formal letter format with all of the sections of a typical business letter, or you may want to modify the letter format to make it more readable and more effective. A letter proposal will not include an executive summary, although it might have one or more appendixes for additional explanatory or background material.

Short Formal Report Format. Many business people use the short formal report format for most of their business proposals. This type of report is printed, usually with a cover sheet, but it has only a few sections, so it does not need a table of contents. The short formal report is usually not bound, nor does it contain some of the extra elements of the formal report, such as appendixes, references, and indexes.

Semi-formal Report Format. If a report becomes long enough to have a Table of Contents and several sections, it may be considered a semi-formal report. This type of report will probably be presented in a three-ring binder or a plastic binder. It may contain one or more appendixes, but it probably does not include other formal report elements, such as an index or a bibliography.

Formal Report Format. A formal report is the most lengthy and detailed type of report. A formal proposal may contain one or more of the following elements:

Front Material

1. **Transmittal Letter.** A transmittal letter is a separate document which is included with a formal report that is presented by mail to a company or organization. The transmittal letter serves to introduce the presenting organization and the report itself. In some cases, the transmittal letter is included within the report, but in most formal reports, the transmittal letter is a separate document.

2. **Cover.** A formal proposal almost always has a front cover and usually a back cover. The cover may be bound or inserted into a clear pocket in the binder.

3. **Title Page.** The title page presents the title of the proposal, the company or individual who is presenting the report, and the company or individual who is receiving the report. Often the date when the proposal is being presented is included, and sometimes the location (city and state) of the presentation.

4. **Executive Summary.** Formal proposals will almost certainly include an executive summary. The more formal and the longer the report, the longer the executive summary will be; an executive summary

in a very long, very formal report may be several pages long. The executive summary may be placed either before or after the table of contents.

5. **Table of Contents.** The table of contents is a necessary part of long, formal reports with several sections and multiple chapters. The table of contents should be generated by your word processing application.

Proposal Body

1. **Page Numbers/Identifier.** As you set up the format for your proposal, be sure to include page numbers and an identifier on each page of the proposal. You will need to use the "Header" and "Footer" feature of your word processing application to insert this information. You can insert the page number at the top right of the pages or the center bottom; either place is acceptable. The identifier should include a briefer form of the title of the proposal, your name or your company's name, and the name of the client. For example, the identifier for a proposal to design a Web site for a law firm may look like this: "Web site Design/ Strickland Law Firm/CharterWebDesign." Also include in the identifier the date of the presentation or the date of delivery of the proposal.

2. **Copyright, Trademark, or Non-Disclosure Statement.** At the bottom of each page of your proposal, you may want to insert a copyright statement or a non-disclosure statement, letting your prospective client know that you consider the material proprietary and protected, and that you own the rights to this material. A copyright statement is presented in the following form:

©2008 Charter Web Design. All Rights Reserved.

The phrase "all rights reserved" is used to clarify your understanding that all rights to use the materials contained in the business proposal, in any form, are retained by you and your company. This would include use of the materials in other media or other formats. See Chapter 8 for a more complete discussion of non-disclosure agreements and their effect on business proposals.

3. **Body of the Proposal.** The various proposal outline formats are discussed earlier in this chapter.

End Material

1. **Reference List/Works Cited/Bibliography.** Many business proposals contain a list of references cited and/or referred to in the production of the document. If you have used external references or interviews in the proposal, be sure you include information about these sources in a listing at the end of the proposal. Chapter 11 contains a more complete discussion of how to cite sources and prepare a reference list.

2. **Appendixes (sometimes called "Appendices").** An appendix is a reference section, which provides additional information on specific subjects within the body of the proposal. Appendixes contain information that may be considered distracting or too detailed for inclusion in the body of the proposal. Appendixes are usually listed with capital letters, such as A., B., C., and so forth. Some common appendixes in a business proposal may be:

   a. Résumés of key individuals responsible for the presentation of the proposal or for the implementation of the project.

   b. Detailed demographic information for marketing and sales purposes.

c. Detailed information about the products or services included in the proposal. For example, a proposal for renovation of an office may include specifications for office furniture, partitions, and office machines.

d. Results of surveys or questionnaires.

e. Transcripts of interviews.

f. Approval letters.

g. Maps, photos, graphics, or illustrations that are too large to be included in the body of the proposal.

3. **Index.** Some long formal proposals include an index, which may be helpful to the client to find information within the body of the proposal. You can generate an index using the "index" feature of your word processing application. To create an index, you must label key words and phrases; the software then notes these key phrases each time they occur in the proposal, and it produces the index, in alphabetical order, on the page you designate. For example, an index for this book may include "non-disclosure agreement," "plagiarism," and "executive summary," and list the page numbers where these subjects are discussed. It is a good idea to create the index items as you go along, noting key terms in your proposal; this will make it easier to produce the index when you have finished the proposal.

CHAPTER 14

THE LETTER OR
MEMO AS PROPOSAL

In the past 15 years, since the advent of the Internet, businesspeople have become adept at writing short and informal reports. Some of these business proposals and reports have come in the form of e-mail, while others take the form of memos and short letters. This section looks at the format and construction of a short business proposal or report.

Memos and e-mail memos are used for many kinds of reports and for informal business proposals. Some informal reports are submitted as attachments to e-mails, while others may be more informal, being placed in the body of the report itself.

Memos follow a specific format. Sometimes the format is dictated by your company, while at other times, you may have the option of creating your own format. The format typically includes:

A heading containing

- To:

- From:

- Subject (or RE, which is short for "Regarding"):

- Date:

A body, containing either numbered paragraphs or regular paragraphs. Here are some suggestions for the format of the body:

- Start with the purpose of the memo.

- Write a sentence or two providing your professional credentials to establish your credibility.

- Go straight to the basic conclusion; do not make the reader have to read all the way to the end to figure out what you want.

- Provide data and research to support your conclusion.

- Include costs and budget.

A conclusion, which wraps up the business proposal and provides the reader with a summary statement.

If you are preparing a short, informal written report in a letter, include the following elements:

- State your objective; you should be able to do this in a sentence (no more than two sentences). Explain why you are writing the proposal letter.

- Provide a context for the proposal, explaining the situation that caused you to make the proposal, or the issues that need to be solved by the proposal.

- Include a discussion of all relevant factors, both pro and con. One way to keep this discussion interesting may be to set up the sections in the form of questions the reader may ask while reviewing this proposal. For example, "Will the new system save money?" or, "How much time will it take before startup on this proposed project?"

Some other types of brief informational business proposals and reports include:

1. *Analytical proposals*, in which several alternatives and situations are analyzed and one is recommended over the others.

2. *Background reports*, which do not make any proposal, but provide organizational or personal statements about the people involved. Sometimes an analytical approach can be an excellent choice for a business executive who does not have time to read the entire report.

3. *Introduction, Methodology, Results, Discussion (IMRD) business reports* provide new knowledge for your reader about a subject. An IMRD may be part of a larger business proposal, or may be a stand-alone report to present the result of some kind of research or investigation.

   • In the introduction, describe what you are investigating and the point you are making (why you are writing this report). To write the introduction, consider the goal of the project and the goal of the report.

   • In the methodology section, describe the process you used to search for and analyze the information. You should also discuss your professional credentials in this section, and explain in detail who you talked to, what investigations you ran, and how you dealt with legal and ethical issues in your research. Be sure you include an explanation of how you tied your work to the goal you wanted to achieve in the project.

- In the research section, describe the results of your work. You should include relevant and meaningful tables and graphs to present your results. Keep these to a minimum, and focus on the one or two graphics that can best portray your results.

- In the discussion section, discuss the implications and significance of the results of your research, relating these results to the question you raised in the introduction. A concluding statement should be part of this section. This section is also the place for any recommendations or proposals for further action.

4. *Progress reports,* which inform others in your company about the progress you have made toward a goal. A progress report can be considered a type of business proposal, because in this report, you often must request additional time or money to continue the project. Progress reports are written with two goals: (a) to get approval by your superiors to continue a project, and (b) to allow you to extend a project or to allocate additional resources to a project. The typical format for a progress report is:

  - Introduction

  - Work Completed

  - Work Scheduled

  - Issues and Concerns

  - Conclusion

In all types of information reports and business proposals, remember:

- Consider your audience, or those multiple audiences who will be reading your report.

- Set a timeline for completing the report and stay with that timeline.

- Even if you have written to this audience before, you must establish (or re-establish) your credibility each time you make a presentation or write a report.

- Follow your outline, including all relevant sections of the report. Forgetting a section will cause your reader(s) to have questions.

- Select and prepare appropriate and meaningful visuals that will enhance the report's effectiveness.

- Write your introduction and conclusion as persuasive pieces, making sure you create interest and desire in the introduction, and a call to action in the conclusion.

- Review your project for grammar, spelling, sentence structure, and ease of reading. Make sure references are cited correctly and appropriately and are from reliable sources.

Letters as Proposals

If you are crafting a proposal in the form of a letter, you have two possibilities to consider when formatting the letter:

Traditional Letter Format. You can set up the format of the letter in a traditional letter format. This format includes:

1. Letterhead. Use your company's letterhead, centered, at the top of the first page of the letter.

2. Date. Insert the date of the presentation or the date you mailed the proposal.

3. Inside Address. Include the name of the individual who will be receiving the report, along with that person's address.

4. Salutation or greeting. In most business proposals, you have already identified the person to whom the proposal is being written, so you can omit the salutation.

5. Body of the letter. Use a modified proposal format:

   a. Introduction and Background

   b. Goals and Objectives

   c. Methods, Tasks, and Timelines

   d. Pricing

   e. Outcomes

   f. Conclusion

6. Closing. You may also want to omit the traditional closing when using letter format for a business proposal.

7. Signature, printed name, and position of the sender. This is an important part of the letter, since it establishes you as the writer and clearly states your intention of being bound by the terms you have set forth in this proposal letter.

In some situations, a business letter may also include the following optional information:

- Carbon Copy Recipients (CC:). Although "carbon copy" is an anachronistic term (no business letters written in the 21st century use carbon paper) this terminology is still in use to list individuals who will receive copies of the document.

- Enclosures (ENC:). Enclosures might include appendixes, references, and résumés of key individuals.

- Reference Initials (of the typist). Typist initials are sometimes omitted in this type of document.

As with longer proposals, be certain to include a header for each page of the proposal letter which includes the name of presenter or presenting company, the date, and the page number. The first page of the proposal letter should not include this information.

Transmittal Letter

In cases where a business proposal is transmitted by mail instead of in person, the proposal may include a transmittal letter. The transmittal letter serves as a cover letter or introductory letter; the format is the same as for other business letters. Included in the letter of transmittal are the following elements:

- **Introduction and Purpose Statement.** The letter should briefly introduce the writer and discuss the purpose of the proposal. In a solicited proposal, the purpose would most likely be to respond to an RFP or an internal request for proposal from executives. For an unsolicited proposal, the writer would state that he or she is writing to present a proposal that the potential customer may find interesting. The unsolicited transmittal is basically a sales letter, because the writer must persuade the reader to continue reading the entire proposal.

- **Details and Significance.** The second section of the transmittal letter presents an overview of the proposal and describes its significance. In an unsolicited proposal, the writer continues the attempt to persuade the reader to read the proposal. The ultimate purpose is to get an interview to discuss the proposal further.

- **Closing.** The closing should express the writer's thanks for reading the letter, and it should also direct the reader to the attached proposal. In most cases, the writer should include contact information, both e-mail and phone.

To be most effective, transmittal letters should be only one page long. Remember, the purpose of the transmittal letter is to introduce the proposal and to get the reader to agree to discuss the proposal further.

CHAPTER 15

FORMATTING AND PREPARING YOUR PROPOSAL FOR PRINTING

You are finally finished with the sections of your proposal, and you are ready to print the document. But before you do that, there are several final tasks to be accomplished:

1. Collecting all the information

2. Formatting the document, with chapters, heading and subheadings, and visuals

3. Proofreading and editing

Choosing a Format

The format you select is usually dependent upon the type of proposal you are writing. For example, the format for a response to an RFP will be different from that of a business plan. Here are some considerations for all types of proposal formats:

- Select a common organization, with consistent:

    - Headings and footers

    - Numbering

- Chapters or sections

- Footnotes, endnotes, and in-page citations for sources

- Captions and numbering for visuals.

- Your heading may include your company name and the page number, while the footer may include a copyright statement or other statement of confidentiality. Whatever you decide to include in these elements, make sure it is consistent throughout the proposal.

- Set up your word processing software to create the headings and footings automatically; do not do this manually. Using the capabilities of your application for these insertions to save time and assure they are consistent throughout the proposal.

- Make your organization apparent to your reader.

- Use short paragraphs (three sentences or less) and use bullets wherever possible to create more visual interest and easier reading.

- Use bold and underlining for emphasis, but sparingly. If everything is emphasized, nothing is emphasized. Be consistent with these formatting elements.

- Use the same type of bullets or numbering throughout the proposal.

- Use large margins and a lot of white space for easier reading.

- Make references to other sections of the proposal easy to understand and to find. For example, if you want your reader to refer to information in Chapter 6, include the exact page number for the reference. You can use the tools available in your word processing application to create a link for this purpose; if the page number changes, the reference will also change.

- Set the left margin of the proposal wide enough to allow the document to be three-hole punched or bound.

Proofreading and the Document

You cannot be sure who will be reading your document; it may be someone who does not know the difference between "its" and "it's." On the other hand, it may be someone who is knowledgeable about grammar, spelling, and punctuation, and who takes them seriously. If you encounter the latter type, you can be at jeopardy of having this person discount your proposal. If a number of people in the client's company are reading your proposal, your chances of encountering this type of "picky" person are increased.

As has been emphasized several times, proofreading a document is a vital task not to be overlooked. The difference between acceptance and rejection of a proposal can be linked directly to the perfection of the writing. Although it may be difficult to imagine, a couple of overlooked typographical errors can mean your proposal will be rejected. You also need to edit and check that everything in the proposal is accurate.

When proofreading, go through the document several times, or have different people read the document, and focus on a different aspect each time. For example, one reading should be for continuity, to make sure that the document "flows" nicely along. Another reading should be for major proofreading errors. A third reading may use the proofreading process described below.

Find an impartial reviewer, someone who has little or no knowledge of the content of your business proposal. Have this person read the entire document, noting questions and concerns. This is an important reading, because the reviewer may catch logic errors, unclear wording, or concepts you may not have been aware of. Do not neglect this part of the proofreading process.

If you have not already done this, turn on the "spell check" feature of your word processing program and go through the document, making sure that all errors are either fixed or discounted for a good reason. Most word processors also have a grammar check; sometimes these provide valuable information that you can use to improve the wording of the document. Look at each grammar suggestion to decide if you want to make the suggested change.

Be aware that a spell check feature will not catch errors in usage between homonyms (word that sound the same but are spelled differently, like "weather" and "whether"), nor will it catch other usage errors if the words are spelled correctly. For example, you may have the word "affect," which is spelled correctly, but the word "effect" may be the correct word in the situation. It is best to have a person who is good with grammar review your document for this type of error.

To recognize proofreading errors:

- Read each page from bottom to top, starting at the last word in each line.

- Place your finger under each word and read silently.

- Make a slit in a sheet of paper to reveal only one line of type at a time.

- Read aloud, pronouncing each word carefully.

Check for accuracy:

- Check the accuracy of all names, places, addresses, figures, and dates.

- Be certain sources are cited correctly, using a standard usage guideline.

Creating a Table of Contents

If your business proposal is more than a few pages long, you should create a table of contents so your client can review the document later and find key sections. Creating a table of contents can be accomplished with the help of a word processing application, like Microsoft Word. To create a table of contents:

1. Go through the document, marking headings. Select chapter headings as "Heading 1" and section headings as "Heading 2." All the examples of each heading should be formatted exactly the same. You probably will not need more than two levels of headings, but you can have as many as you want.

2. Position your cursor at the point in the document where you want to insert the table of contents.

3. Then, go to the Format menu and select "References" and "Table of Contents." You can select the number of levels you want to include and the style of table. Then click "OK" and the table will be created.

4. If you make changes to the document after the table of contents is created, you can update the table easily. Use the right click on your mouse to bring up a menu; select the item with the red exclamation point, "Update Table," and choose the "Update Entire Table" option.

Creating a Proposal Cover

Most formal reports include a cover. The cover provides information about the proposal and the person or organization who is presenting the proposal. Even more important than the text is the effect of the layout and color of the cover. The cover is the first thing your reader will see, so it must be both interesting and meaningful. Although the cover is not the most important factor in the success of your proposal, it plays a role in attracting your reader's attention and creating interest. As discussed in Chapter 21, the AIDA formula works to achieve a sale. Your cover provides the attention-getting factor, and it also creates interest in your proposal.

Using the Cover to Sell Your Proposal

Many businesses use original artwork depicting their company on the cover of their business proposals, but you may want to be more innovative and use an illustration or photo. You can decide to put your company logo, colors, and tagline on the cover, but this is probably not the most effective way to sell your customer on your proposal. Instead, use an illustration or photo that makes a statement about the problem you will solve through your proposal.

Create a picture in the reader's mind of what their company will look like after you have finished the proposal and the project. For example, if you are writing a proposal to design a new building for the client, provide artwork showing the new building. If your proposal is for new office furniture, create an illustration showing what the new office will look like. If your proposal relates to increased profits, find an illustration that allows the customer to envision the effect of these profits on company growth, and her own personal success. The more powerful the visual you create, the better your client will be able to "see" the positive effect of your proposal on his organization.

Binding the Proposal

Along with the cover, the binding of your business proposal is the first thing the potential customer sees. Depending on the formality of your proposal, there are a variety of binding types and styles you can use. Here is just a brief sample of these binding types:

- **Three-Ring Binder.** The three-ring binder is one of the most commonly used forms of binding for business proposals and reports. It is easy to use and comes in several different widths for different types of proposals. Some three-ring binders have a clear pocket cover to enable you to insert your own cover page. Others include internal pockets to use for extra papers, computer printouts, and other additional documents. There are a wide variety of styles and colors of three-ring binders.

- **Clear Plastic (Poly) Covers.** You may have used a clear plastic back and front cover with a plastic spine for school reports; many businesses also use these covers for proposals. They work best for shorter, more informal types of reports.

- **Pressboard or Clamp Binders.** This type of binder is usually made of heavy cardboard and contains clamps which hold the pages of the proposal together. This type of binder works best for short reports.

- **Plastic Comb or Spiral Binders.** In this type of binding, you prepare a front and back cover and use a machine to cut out the holes through which the comb or spiral spine fits. Comb bindings open and close to insert the covers and pages; spiral binding is inserted in one operation; both are inserted by machines.

CHAPTER 16

THE EXECUTIVE SUMMARY

At the beginning of your business proposal, you need to insert an executive summary. This section is a separate document because it summarizes all of the elements of your proposal. Although the executive summary is placed at the beginning of the document, it is written last to be sure it incorporates all of the key points you have worked on in the body of your proposal.

An executive summary is one of the most important portions of your business proposal, and it should be constructed carefully, to be certain that it achieves maximum effectiveness. The executive summary has several purposes:

- It captures the client's attention and creates an interest in the entire proposal. In other words, it sells the reader on the idea of reading the full proposal.

- It summarizes the key points in the proposal document in capsule form. Usually an executive summary will use bullet points to lay out these key points, with short examples.

- It tells the story of the proposal, including the "ending," so the reader knows the purpose of the proposal.

- It spells out the conclusion or the "bottom line," answering the question: "What are you proposing and how much will it cost?"

In many companies, several levels of management and executives will review the proposal. The top-level executives may look only at the executive summary and not the entire document, so it is important that this piece is included. You need to write your executive summary to appeal primarily to the top-level executive, but you also need to be sure everyone in the company understands and appreciates this section of your proposal.

The format of your executive summary depends upon the type of business proposal you are creating. If you create a proposal to sell a product or service to a client, you use a sales format for your executive summary; if you create a business plan proposal, you use a different type of format. For a proposal that is responding to an RFP, you need to follow the format of the RFP. This section discusses the various formats for executive summaries.

It is difficult to estimate how long the executive summary may be. In a short business plan proposal, this section may be only one page long. In other, more complex, proposals, the executive summary may be two or three pages long, with subheadings, visuals, and tables.

Executive Summary — Sales Format

When you put together the executive summary for a sales proposal, you may be tempted to use a traditional format for your executive summary, but remember you need to capture your reader's attention first. Avoid starting with a purpose statement, problem statement, overview, or with a lengthy background statement. It is easy to write this way, but it does not serve your purpose of winning acceptance for your proposal.

Begin the executive summary with the endpoint. That is, begin with your recommendation, your conclusion about how to solve the client's problem, or a major point or consideration that will draw the reader in to read more. Here are several examples of good beginning statements in executive summaries:

- *A strong safety plan can benefit your company by providing increased confidence by employees, greater compliance with governmental regulations, and better products for your customers.*

- *Providing your employees with an HSA-type health benefit package can pay off in increased employee loyalty and lower benefit costs for you.*

Note how these statements have the effect of "grabbing" the reader; they call attention to the problem that needs to be solved, and state the benefits to be attained by the company in solving the problem. In essence, this statement creates a "summary within a summary." It calls for your best writing, because you must distill the essence of the entire proposal into one statement. It shows your reader not only that you understand her problem, but that you have the solution to the problem.

After writing the strong introductory sentence, you can proceed to provide more details, including:

- Overview

- Purpose

- Proposal

- Conclusions

Executive Summary — Government Proposal

Proposals to state or federal governments or other governmental entities often are responses to RFPs. In these circumstances, your proposal will usually follow the same format as the RFP, and the executive summary will mirror the proposal. One common executive summary format for governmental proposals is:

- Background

- Scope (discussion of items from RFP)

- Schedule

- Staff

- Budget

- Supporting information

Executive Summary — Business Plan

An executive summary for a business plan serves the important purpose of creating an interest on the part of your banker or lender. Like other kinds of business proposals, a business plan may be read by several individuals within the bank hierarchy, and the top-level bank executives may only see the executive summary. For this reason, you must write the executive summary to provide all the necessary information, including your funding request. Here is one common format for the executive summary for a business plan:

- Describe your company and its products or services.

- Include the mission statement of your company. (See the next section to find information on how to write a mission statement.)

- Describe the people who are managing your company; include a brief statement of credentials (background and experience) for these people.

- Provide a summary description of the market area for your products or services, and describe the target customers to whom you are marketing.

- Include a brief discussion of your competition within this market.

- Discuss your business operations and how your business will be conducted (online, for example) and how sales and customer service will be handled.

- Finally, include your financial projections, with a statement about the funding you are requesting and how you expect to pay it back.

Suggestions for Effective Executive Summaries

No matter what format you use for the executive summary, consider these suggestions for improving its effectiveness:

- Keep the executive summary short and to-the-point.

- Avoid providing too many details; list the key points in bulleted lists and leave the details for the main part of the proposal.

- Keep graphics to a minimum. If there is one key graphic that provides an overview or gives the reader the most important information, include it. Otherwise, save the graphics for the proposal.

- Write to interest several levels of readers. As stated previously, the top-level executives are the target audience for this section, but other readers should also find it interesting and informative.

- If possible, start with an attention-getting statement or question to draw the readers into the document.

- Present benefits and value statements clearly at the beginning of the executive summary. Then, briefly list your supporting statements to show that you are capable of providing these benefits.

- Use positives; avoid negative statements.

- Follow the wishes of the client in listing costs. Some clients request costs be listed separately, particularly in government proposals. In the executive summary for a business plan, on the other hand, you should include your specific loan request.

Finally, before you include the executive summary in your business proposal document, have someone who is unfamiliar with your company and your business read the document for understanding. The reader should be able to understand the main concepts of your business proposal from reading the executive summary. Ask the person to tell you, "What is this proposal about?" "What are the benefits to the company of accepting this proposal?" and "Does the proposal answer all of your questions?" Remember the executive summary is a stand-alone document and must include all of the key points of your business proposal.

CHAPTER 17

MISSION STATEMENTS IN PROPOSALS

The Purpose of Mission Statements

If you have a new company or business, consider constructing a mission statement. Even if your business has been in existence for some time and you have not constructed a mission statement, you should do this. What is a mission statement and why should you put one together?

Your mission statement is the "what" behind your business. Your mission statement describes what you are all about, your company's reason for being in business. You may consider your mission statement to be your "constitution." A mission statement is important to give your stakeholders (those who have a stake in your business, like customers, employees, and shareholders) a meaningful statement about the business. The mission statement encourages your employees to be more committed to the company; it informs and encourages your customers to get involved in your success, and it encourages your shareholders to continue to be committed to the company.

As you construct your mission statement, consider these questions:

- What statement does your mission statement make about your organization's reason to exist?

- How will your company succeed?

- Does the mission statement address the needs of the company's stakeholders?

- Does the mission statement motivate your employees and inspire your customers and shareholders?

Writing and Presenting a Mission Statement

Here are some suggestions to consider as you put together your mission statement:

- Create positive, present, and future statements to set the correct tone for this statement, using words like "will" and "are."

- Refer to your company in the first person plural, "we," to give the mission statement a personal tone.

- Consider the "focus" of your company, including your USP (see Chapter 6).

- Think about areas in which your company specializes.

- Consider how you want to treat employees, and how you would describe their value to the company.

- Consider how you would describe your relationship to your customer.

- Think about the principles to which your company is dedicated. What are the ideals your company holds up to employees as important?

- Consider your long-term commitment to your business, your industry, and your shareholders.

Using Mission Statements to Enhance Your Business Proposal

Now that you have created a mission statement, how can you use it to make your business proposal more effective?

- Share your mission statement with your team before you present your first proposal to inspire them up and give them motivation as they go into the presentation.

- Use the mission statement in your introduction to help establish your credibility and provide your customer with a better understanding of your company. Mission statements can be powerful persuaders.

- Provide a copy of your mission statement in an attractive format on a special page in your proposal so it stands out and creates interest with your audience.

CHAPTER 18

USING CASE STUDIES
IN BUSINESS PROPOSALS

A case study can be an effective addition to a business proposal. Depending upon the type of proposal you are writing, a case study can serve several purposes:

1. The case study can show your client how you work, the processes you use, and how you complete assignments.

2. If you are able to get permission from the client whose case study you are using, you can add to your credibility by showing how successful you were in previous similar projects. In essence, the case study serves as a testimonial from the other client.

3. The case study shows your client you understand his needs by your selection of case study to match the current prospective client's needs.

4. The case study gives the prospect the ability to visualize herself in a position of success at the end of the case. Giving a client a vision of how successful the project will be is a great way to "seal the deal."

5. The case study will relieve the anxieties of the prospective client, allowing him to see that the process was painless and not as overwhelming as first imagined.

Here are the steps in creating and using a case study in your business proposal:

1. Find a suitable case study. You need to find one of your best clients or customers and ask permission to write about them and their experience of working with you and your company. If you cannot get permission, you can use a "blind" case, but this is not as effective as one with a name on it.

   Select a case study in which the client and the circumstances are as close as possible to the circumstances in the prospect's case. You want the prospect to see exactly what she will receive in services and outcomes.

2. Prepare the case study using one of the following organizational styles:

   a. Write a chronological case study in which you discuss the client's company from the time you began the project until its completion. The advantage to this style is that the prospective client can see how you take a client through the process of accepting, starting, progressing through, and completing a project.

   b. Write the case study in a problem and solution format. In other words, describe the client's problem and the work that needed to be done to fix the problem, and then describe how you and your company solved the client's problem.

3. Do not hesitate to include direct quotes from the former client or praise from top executives in the company. If you cannot get direct quotes, see if you can persuade the client to let you write a testimonial to include within the case study; of course, you should give him the chance to review and edit anything you have written.

4. Focus your description of the case primarily on the processes you went through, not secondarily on individuals or areas within the client's company. You want your prospective client to see how the process worked, but you also want the client to see how well you worked with the people at the client location. Keep individual names, titles, and job descriptions to a minimum, unless you have a great working relationship with the previous client.

5. Conclude your case study with a strong ending, providing details about how the client in the case was successful; how you saved the client money; or how you increased revenue, sales, or marketing. The more details about the outcome you include, the better, so the client can see herself in the position of the case study client, becoming successful and reaping the rewards of a great relationship.

The case study should include an introduction, a summary, a body, and a conclusion. The case study may be inserted directly into the business proposal as a chapter, or it may be included as an appendix at the end of the proposal.

Here is a sample outline and format for a case study to include in your business proposal:

- **Introduction.** In this section, you should briefly outline the background for the case study.

- **Summary.** Like an executive summary, this section should present all the information in the case study, from beginning to end. Include a conclusion, summarizing the benefits the client experienced from working with you and your company.

- **Profile of the Client.** Write a brief description of the client and his company, including company history, key individuals in the company, and major products and services. You may also want to include details about the company's income and sales, if these figures are important to your case.

- **Problem.** Discuss the problem the client was experiencing that caused her to need your services. Provide as much detail as necessary to create a story of the situation. If the company prepared an RFP, include details on what they were requesting in the document.

- **Vendor Selection.** Include information from the clients about why they selected your company above others. Have the clients describe the benefits they saw initially in selecting your service or product, particularly if you were not the low bidder on the project.

- **Solution.** Spend time describing how you solved the client's problem. Include quotes from various key individuals within the company who worked with you to solve the problem. Have them tell how they liked working with you and how long it took to solve the problem and bring the project to resolution. The more detail you include in this section, the better your prospect will be able to see how he can benefit from working with you.

CHAPTER 19

USING VISUALS IN PROPOSALS

A business proposal without visuals may be good, but it will not be as interesting. This section of the book will describe the types of visuals you may want to include, and you will be able to see how to make your visuals more effective and more interesting.

As you plan your business proposal, make notes about key pieces of information that may be enhanced by turning them into visuals. You may not be able to include all the visuals you plan, but the more you have, the better chance you have of finding visuals that will enhance your proposal.

Why Use Visuals?

Visuals are used in business proposals for a number of reasons:

Visuals Improve Understanding of the Subject

Visuals like photos, diagrams, line drawings, full views, and breakout views of products can give your client more information than a written description. Consider the following:

"A foramen is a hole in the skull." Telling you about a foramen is meaningless if you have never seen one. Now consider this:

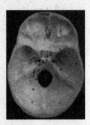

(Source: http://en.wikipedia.org/w/index.php?title=Foramen&oldid=142641874)

Providing an image of the subject gives more information and makes the reader more comfortable with her understanding.

Visuals Summarize and Clarify Complex Technical Data

Many business proposals include financial spreadsheets for this purpose. In a business plan, for example, a "sources and uses of funds" statement provides an overview and summary of the financial requirements and funds provided and needed by the business owner.

If you were to write out the details of this statement, you may write it like this:

For startup, this business will require $196,176 in funds for startup equipment, $1,144 in funds for initial quantities of supplies and advertising materials, $34,325 in funds for facilities costs, and $8,585 in funds for other startup costs. In total, for all of the startup requirements, a term loan in the amount of $240,230 is requested. In addition, the company will require a working capital line of credit in the amount of $123,166. The total startup funding required is $363,396.

The owner expects to be able to contribute $20,047, of which $13,047 is in the form of supplies and equipment and $7,000 is in the form of personal cash. This leaves a total of $207,136 in term loan and $123,166 in working capital needs, which are requested from the lender.

In contrast, here is the same information in the form of a sources and uses of funds statement:

STARTUP SOURCES AND USES OF FUNDS STATEMENT	
Uses of Funds	
Startup Assets: Equipment	$ 196,176
Startup Assets: Supplies/Advertising	$ 1,144
Startup Facilities Costs	$ 34,325
Other Startup Costs	$ 8,585
Term Loan Amount:	$ 240,230
Working Capital Line of Credit	$ 123,166
Total Funds Required	$ 363,396
Sources of Funds	
Owner-provided Funds:	
Owner-provided Cash for Term Loan	$ 20,047
Startup Equipment, Supplies, etc.	$ 13,047
Personal Savings	$ 7,000
Bank Financing — Term Loan	$ 207,136
Bank Financing — Working Capital	$ 123,166
Total Sources of Funds	$ 363,396

The information provided by the sources and uses of funds statement is clearer and more easily readable than the narrative form. You should use financial documents wherever possible in your business proposal, keeping them short and to the point.

Visuals Add Interest to Your Proposal and to Your Presentation

Well-placed and interesting photos of key individuals within your company can be effective in giving a personal touch to your proposal. Use photos, sketches, drawings, and logos if you want to create a certain image of your company. For example, if you use a small logo on each page of your business proposal, you will create a subconscious reinforcement of your company in the customer's mind.

Graphics Add Interest to Your Proposal

Here is a graphic from a PowerPoint presentation that was part of a proposal for a leadership development program at a college. Note how the elements of the proposal are more interesting in graphic format.

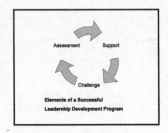

Visuals Help Reinforce the Most Important Points in Your Business Proposal

Photos are powerful memory tools. For example, photos of a client's workplace before and after a restoration project you worked on can help establish your ability to do the work.

> **To insert a graphic into an application,** use the "Cut" and "Paste" features. You can use this method to transfer a graphic from any application to any other, as long as both applications are in a Windows-based system. For example, you can "Cut" a graphic from Excel and insert it into Word or PowerPoint.
>
> Simply highlight the graphic and "Cut" it from one application, then "Paste" it into the second application.
>
> If you need to re-size the image, click on the image to bring up the "handles" around the image and bring up the picture toolbar.

Types of Visuals

Here are some of the most common visual aids used in business proposals, with examples of each type:

- **Tables.** Tables are lists in graphic format. They present information in a form that can be read and analyzed easily. Tables are a good way to present large amounts of information or to find information easily. Tables are arranged in columns and rows.

- **Graphs.** Graphs are used in proposals to represent relationships between data and trends over time. A temperature graph, for example, shows the changes in average high and low temperatures in a city each month for a year. While a table could represent the same information, it is much easier to see the trends with a graph.

  Graphs come in several types: line, bar, and pie.

  Line graphs are best used to show trends over time, or relationships between two variables. For example, the graph below is a line graph showing changes in average daily temperature each month for a year. Another type of line graph is useful in comparing two variables. One variable is placed on the horizontal and is considered the "x" variable; the second variable is placed on the vertical and is considered the "y" variable.

  In the example below, it is easy to see the variations in monthly temperature, both normal low and high temperatures, in the city of Walla Walla, Washington over one year.

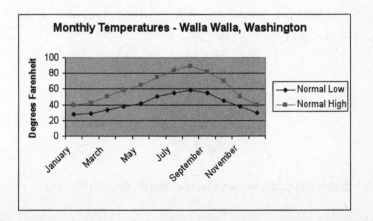

Bar graphs are commonly used to compare and contrast several similar items, and they are useful because they can be used to compare a number of items simultaneously. For example, you may use a bar graph to compare the levels of education of several countries, or the increases in office rental prices over time for several cities.

Here is the same information on the normal high and low temperatures of Walla Walla, Washington over a year, presented in bar graph format:

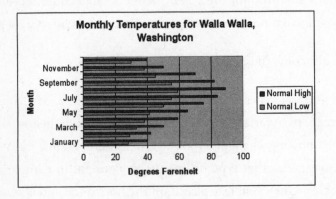

Pie graphs or charts are used primarily to show the relative size of various parts of a whole entity. For example, you may see a pie chart showing the amount of your tax dollar which is spend on military, domestic, and other programs. In using a pie chart, all elements must add up to 100 percent. For this reason, it has a limited use, but is helpful in presentations to readers who are less sophisticated. For example, here is a pie chart showing the populations of English native speakers in various countries in 1997:

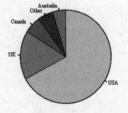

Source: http://en.wikipedia.org/wiki/Image:English_dialects1997.svg

In creating these charts, there are a few important things to remember:

1. Match the type of chart to the data being presented. A line graph may be the best way to present data over time, but it may not be useful in showing comparisons between various entities.

2. Consider how the graph will look when it is printed and used in a presentation. In some cases, a proposal may be printed in black and white rather than color, and a bar graph or pie chart may lose the required detail to show relationships.

3. In using line graphs, consider the high and low points and match to the highest and lowest data being presented. For example, if the smallest number on the vertical is $1 million, do not start with $1.

4. Keep graphs simple. Some people like to use three-dimensional graphs, but they are too complex for most people to view and understand easily.

Charts are another common form of visual, and they also come in various types. Charts may also be called diagrams or figures; most often they refer to figures that show relationships or that represent processes and procedures.

One common form of chart is the flow chart, which is used to show processes or decision points. Flow charts are easy to understand and contain common elements, including boxes and arrows, to show the flow of a decision or process.

Another business chart is the organization chart, which is used to show relationships in a business or other organization:

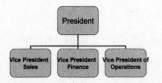

Usually, an organization chart includes only the top two or three layers of management, but some are more complex, showing more layers.

Presenting Visuals within Your Proposal

It is important to remember that there are specific requirements for the numbering and presentation of visuals within your business report. Each visual must have:

1. A clear, meaningful title. The title should include enough information so the reader can immediately grasp the entire meaning of the table. For example, a table titled "Life Expectancy" is not adequate. A title "Life Expectancy of Individuals Based on Current Age" may be better.

2. A sequential number so the reader can locate it. In some cases, the numbers are distinct to each chapter. For example, the first visual in Chapter 2 may be Figure 2.1. This aids the reader in finding the visual within the document.

3. An explanation of the purpose of the visual, along with the sequential number. For example, Figure 2.1 may include a descriptive statement, "A sample sources and uses of funds statement." This explanation helps the reader understand why the visual is included and its purpose.

Increasing Effectiveness of Visuals

When you are creating visuals, keep in mind the key elements that must be considered with every visual, whether it is a graphic, a table, or a drawing.

- Simplicity. Keep the presentation of each visual as simple as possible so it will be easily understandable to your reader. Tables, for example, can be complicated and difficult to understand. You may need to focus on just one portion of a table, or to re-draw a table to eliminate any unnecessary elements, to make the table more simple. For example, if you are using a bar graph, you may need to eliminate some unnecessary bars that do not add to the point you are trying to make. Although you will be providing a title and additional explanatory material with each visual, the meaning of every visual should be immediately apparent to your reader, no matter what level of understanding this person has.

- Emphasis. Visuals should be selected to emphasize specific points you want to make in your business proposal. Remember that if you emphasize everything, you emphasize nothing; select visuals carefully to emphasize major points or to clarify the most important concepts. Having too many visuals is worse than not having enough. Your reader or audience assumes that you will be using visuals to support your most important points. Therefore, present the key items in each visual in the most prominent way, through color, position, size, or other means. Visually downplay the less important items. For example, you may want to highlight a column in a table that shows the most important information about company profits.

- Unity. Each visual should contain one central message that supports your proposal. Visuals should not be added just for "effect," but each should clearly support your objective and increase the effectiveness of your proposal.

- Consistency. Develop a plan for using visuals in your proposal. Each visual should be in a logical place in relation to the text; caption visuals consistently and number them in order. Make it easy for your reader to find and read your visuals.

Here are some additional points to keep in mind as you consider including visuals in your business proposal:

- Plan where to include visuals as you prepare the report; look for opportunities to include visuals at points of emphasis. Do not wait until you have finished and then add the visuals.

- Look at visuals on the pages before you print the document. Avoid having a visual show across two pages; if necessary, place the visual on the second page and leave white space on the previous page.

- Consider the expectations and cultural biases of your reader as you select visuals. Culture, education, and other experiences condition people to expect things to look certain ways, and these expectations may affect the way they respond to your visuals. For example, green is associated with money in the United States, but not in some foreign countries.

CHAPTER 20

PRESENTING YOUR PROPOSAL

Planning the Presentation

You have completed your business proposal, printed it, and have an appointment to present your proposal to a client. The next step is to plan the presentation. You need to think carefully about a number of factors that can influence what you present and how you present it.

First, think carefully about your audience and how you should structure your presentation. What you have discovered about the personality of the person who will be making the decision may influence the type of presentation you will provide. If your client is "high-tech" and computer literate, a PowerPoint presentation may be expected. For a small business owner or professional who is not interested in technology, a one-on-one presentation may be all you need. If you are not sure what type of presentation your client prefers, ask early in the discussion. Consider making your presentation as simple as possible; many clients appreciate a simple and direct presentation. In addition to the PowerPoint presentation, you may want to consider a series of posters or other printed materials. Presenting in a format that makes your client comfortable is an important consideration when planning how to present your proposal.

Second, consider the environment in which you will be presenting the proposal and the number of people in the audience. If you are in a conference room with the latest equipment, of if you are presenting to a large group of people, you will probably be able to do a great PowerPoint presentation. For a one-person presentation, you may want to walk the person through your proposal, answering questions, and providing a summary. If the location is a small store, a factory, or warehouse, you may not be in a position to use a PowerPoint format. In these cases, you have to improvise to accommodate the location.

Third, consider the principle of continuity. Your audience sees a series of visual aids as a whole and assumes that you will use the elements of design in a consistent manner from one slide or poster to another.

Overcoming Your Fear of Presenting

Many people have a strong fear of public speaking. In fact, according to *The Book of Lists* (Wallace and Wallachinsky, 1997), fear of public speaking (also called "glossophobia," or stage fright) is the number-one fear in most polls; more people are afraid of public speaking than of death. In the world of business, it is almost impossible to avoid public speaking, particularly if your job requires you to participate in presenting business proposals.

If you have spoken in business or professional situations before, you may have experienced the emotions and physical sensations of fear — dry mouth, lightheadedness, queasy stomach, sweaty palms, and more. These reactions are not unusual for untrained speakers, but you need to overcome them if you want the presentation to be effective.

If this is your first presentation of a business proposal, you need to work on overcoming your nervousness and fear so your presentation will be effective. To help you relax and conquer your fear, there are some techniques you can use.

- Be prepared. Be certain you are comfortable with the content of your speech and with your delivery.

- Focus on your presentation and not your audience. Novice speakers are focused on themselves and their fear. As soon as you decide to concentrate on the message you want to deliver, you will find that your fear lessens and you become more confident.

- Have notes ready to use in case you forget what you want to say.

- Smile. Look at your audience as friends and not enemies. Some experts tell you to picture the audience without any clothes on; they suggest this to get you to see the audience as less intimidating and more human. If this helps, that is fine, but it may be better to find a few friendly faces in the audience and focus on them as you begin. In any group of more than two people, you find someone who is a "head nodder" or a person who smiles, who appears interested in what you are saying and wants you to succeed. If you do not think this person will be in your audience, ask a friend to sit in on the presentation to provide this agreeable person.

- Relax before you start. Take a deep breath, think about your opening, and begin. You will find that as you get into your topic and work through the points of your presentation, your nervousness will decrease and you may start to enjoy yourself.

- Be positive. Your audience wants you to succeed. They also want to hear what you are saying and, if you have done your job well up to this point, they are certain you have something worthwhile to say. Do not sell yourself short; assume you will succeed.

- Visualize success. One of the most powerful factors in success in any profession is the ability of successful people to visualize themselves succeeding. Professional golfers, for example, spend a great deal of time practicing, but they also spend a lot of time imagining how they will play the game. They visualize themselves addressing the ball, hitting the ball, watching the ball land in the best spot, and getting a low score. You can do the same thing. In the days before you give your presentation, take time to close your eyes and visualize in detail the way your presentation will progress. Imagine yourself stepping up to the front of the room and greeting your client and others. Move step by step through the presentation, thinking about what you will say and how it will be received by your audience. At the end, imagine yourself giving a powerful closing message and having your speech enthusiastically applauded. This may sound silly, but it works. If nothing else, it will provide you with the confidence you need to be at your best in the presentation.

- Finally, and most importantly, practice. The best way to overcome fear of speaking is to practice until you are confident. Practice techniques are discussed below.

Be prepared. You need to be prepared in two ways: with the language of the presentation and with the speaking skills you will use. After you put together the formal presentation (PowerPoint, slides, posters, or other media) you need to carefully consider what you will say at every point. Some speakers use note cards, writing down every word they say. In this situation, you do not want to be reading note cards, because this looks unprofessional and interferes with your ability to look at your audience.

On the other hand, do not try to memorize the presentation. If you get hung up on a point and cannot remember what to say, you will look unprepared and you will have to refer to notes anyway. One trick many teachers use is to rely on the prompts from the presentation to lead you through your talk. The PowerPoint slides or posters can be your notes, helping you to remember what you want to say about each slide. That is why having good visuals for your presentation is so important.

Be prepared for questions. Consider the possible questions your listeners may ask. If you are working on this presentation with colleagues, spend time asking each other possible questions. Be as outrageous as possible and evaluate each other on your answers. Some of the most impossible questions may be asked, and you must be prepared for them. This is one case where your knowledge of the client is vital. Thinking about what kinds of questions your client may ask is critical.

Consider how you will handle questions during your presentation. In most cases, you will have a limited time to give the presentation, so you may not want to take questions during this time. On the other hand, some executives have a habit of breaking in with questions, and you will need to answer those, but do so quickly and then return to the presentation. If you have provided handouts with your presentation, you may want to have people take the handouts before you begin talking, so your audience can take notes while you are talking. This is the most effective way to use handouts for a proposal presentation. If you wait until the presentation is over before you distribute handouts, you will find that your audience is scrambling to try to find something to write on to take notes, which is more distracting and gives your audience a feeling that you are unprepared.

Be prepared with your equipment and the room. If you have not spoken in this room before, arrive there at least 15 minutes early so you can prepare. Make certain everything works. It is not going to win your client's approval if you have a great presentation but you cannot give it because you are not able to get the video projector to work.

Check everything in the room, including the heat and light. Make certain everyone in the room will be able to see your presentation easily. If you can, sit in all of the chairs that people will be using to verify their line of sight. If the lights are too bright for people to see your PowerPoint, do not hesitate to turn off a few. If you cannot, you may want to consider changing to a darker background for your PowerPoint slides (more on that later) so they can be seen more easily.

In short, being prepared means leaving nothing to chance. Murphy's Law of Audiovisuals states that "if anything can go wrong in a presentation, it will, and at the worst possible time." After all of your great work on this proposal and your effort in preparing a presentation, you do not want anything to keep you from your goal of an award-winning proposal.

Plan your practice schedule. Follow this suggested outline for practicing your presentation and you will find that you are well prepared, confident, and relaxed:

- First, write the entire script for your presentation, using the material from your PowerPoint slides as references. Add notes on places where you want to pause or make your voice louder or softer, talk more slowly, move your arms or your body, or move across the room. In other words, prepare a complete script of your presentation to follow.

- Practice once with the script in front of you, deliberately making gestures, varying your voice, and moving. Go through the entire presentation in this manner.

- Go through the presentation a second time, using the script as little as possible. At this point you may want to make index cards to use as prompts. Do not get too attached to these cards, because you probably will not use them for the final presentation.

- After you have gone through your presentation several times, there are a couple of possibilities to help you refine your presentation. You could have someone do a video of your presentation, playing it back for you so you can see everything, and so you can analyze the presentation for improvement points.

- Consider having someone (or several people) listen to your presentation. Having two or more people listen is helpful because each of them can be listening for different things. For example, one person may listen for content and understanding, and ask the question, "Is what the speaker says enjoyable and understandable?" The second listener may pay attention to distractions, like mannerisms, vocal "tics" or non-words, and the speed and volume of your voice. Listeners should make notes on what they hear so they can discuss them with you at the end of the presentation.

- Time your presentation. Make it as short as possible to present all of the relevant information you need to impart. If you promise a client that you will talk no longer than 20 minutes, make sure you are finished within that time frame. A long presentation is more detrimental to your success than a short one. A perfectly timed presentation adds to your credibility and to your chances of acceptance.

Practice. To give an effective presentation, you need to practice your language, vocal elements, movements, and other nonverbal expressions. For example:

- Vary the volume of your voice at appropriate points, getting louder for emphasis or softer to get the audience's attention.

- Change the speed at which you talk. In most cases, nervous speakers talk too fast. Slow down when you talk, so you can connect with your listeners better and give them time to think about what you have said.

- Consider variations in your arm movements to emphasize key points in your presentation.

- Practice making eye contact with your listeners.

- Practice body movement and walking, if that is possible. If not, make certain that you do not move continuously in a swaying motion or back and forth motion; these kinds of repetitive movements can distract your audience from the subject of your presentation.

- Plan pauses for dramatic effect. Pausing is a great way to get your audience's attention and make certain the next words they hear are listened to.

- Talk loudly enough to be heard by all of your listeners. The best way to assure that you are heard is to talk one row beyond your last listener. For example, if your audience is seated around a conference table, direct your voice behind the people furthest away from you. Imagine someone sitting behind the CEO or the business owner. That way, you can be heard by everyone sitting closer than this person.

Creating the Presentation

The most important keys to an effective business proposal presentation are:

1. Keep it short. Include everything you must include to win acceptance of the proposal and nothing else. How long should a presentation be? You should be able to make your point, even with slides, in 20 minutes or less, and most listeners begin to "tune out" after about 15 minutes. Use this time period as the guideline for your presentation. Unless there is some overwhelming reason why your presentation must be longer, try to keep it to 20 minutes or less.

2. Keep it simple. A confused person does not buy. If you try to present too much material, your client will shake his head and smile, but you may lose the sale because the person is overwhelmed with the substance of your talk. Keep the charts and graphs to a minimum;

find the ones that most dramatically make your case and save the others for the client to read in the proposal document.

3. Keep it organized. Make sure the presentation flows logically from beginning to middle to end. This subject will be discussed in more detail below, but consider the classic format for speeches:

   a. *First, tell them what you are going to tell them.* Introduce your listeners to the subject you will be talking about, and the one main point you want to emphasize. Make it clear to your listeners exactly what they will hear, and make sure that everything in the speech relates to that point.

   b. *Then, tell them.* Discuss your main subject, using verbal "bullet points" and examples to take your reader through your presentation. Use transition words and phrases like, "first," "second," "then," "and also," "finally," and "in conclusion."

   c. *Finally, tell them what you've told them.* In your conclusion, summarize your main point for your listeners. Give them a capsule version of your main points, in order. Then provide a final "call to action" or emphatic concluding statement at the end.

4. Keep it interesting. Whatever visuals you use should enhance the interest level of your presentation. Include an example or an impressive chart or table to keep your client at the edge of his seat and ready to say "yes."

Outline Your Presentation

You may initially decide to base the presentation on the structure of your written proposal. Your client can read the entire proposal later, but you want to be certain you have her attention, have created a desire on the client's part for your proposal, and have a clear "call to action" at the end to close the sale.

You should include the most important elements of the proposal, but the presentation should follow a different structure. The key to structuring an effective proposal is to hit the highlights, giving your clients just enough to make them eager to read the document and accept your proposal. The mistake made by many professionals is trying to restate the entire business proposal in the presentation. If you attempt this, you will lose your audience and you will have lost the most important items you want your client to remember so he is motivated to accept your proposal.

Before you outline your presentation, go back to your original planning for the business proposal and consider the key points and the value proposition you wanted to portray. Answer the question: "If I were this client, why would I want to accept this proposal?" Then list key benefits, with supporting examples for each. Spending time on this step is important; do not begin your presentation outline until you have completed this exercise.

Consider this outline for your presentation:

- Capture the audience's attention. Start with a powerful and interesting opening to engage your audience immediately in what you are saying. This kind of opening can incorporate a deliberately shocking statement or question, or it can create a sense of urgency in your audience. For example, you may begin by providing a fact about the client's company that shows the problem within the organization.

- Tell the audience the purpose of your presentation. In other words, tell them what you are going to tell them. At the end of the presentation, what do you want them to do? You want them to accept your proposal, but be specific about what this means. If you are dealing with a hostile or unreceptive audience, you may not want to be this direct (see Chapter 4), but, in most cases, the audience will appreciate your directness and honesty.

- Briefly establish your credentials. If the client is not familiar with you or your company, take a few minutes to talk about your background and experience. Do not spend too much time on this because you must move on to the important matter of persuading the client that you have the answer to his problem. The client can read more about your credentials in the document you have prepared.

- Move into the body of your presentation, using key points to make your case. In this portion of the presentation:

  o Tell stories. Make a point, and then tell a story to illustrate it. For example, if you are describing how your services will improve the client's sales, tell about another client whose sales improved after they used your services. Keep these stories to a minimum; a few is enough to make your point.

  o Provide evidence. Use charts, tables, graphs, and other meaningful visuals from your proposal to substantiate the benefits of your proposal for the client. Again, keep these to a minimum. You do not have time to use many examples, and you can direct the client to read the entire proposal to find additional examples.

  o Use the most compelling examples and stories first, in case you run out of time. If you plan the presentation correctly, you should have time for all of your examples, but if the client asks questions, you may be rushed at the end. If you have the most important examples last, you may have to skip them; it is better to skip the least important ones.

- Conclude with a "call to action." Summarize the benefits to the client of accepting your proposal. Then answer the "so what" question and tell them what you want them to do. In other words, close the sale by asking the closing question you have decided on. For example, ask, "Would you like to take advantage of our special pricing and sign the agreement today?" Or say, "We can promise delivery by the first of April if you sign the agreement today."

- Thank the client for her attention. Then stop. Resist the impulse to say anything else, like "What do you think?" or "I guess that is it." If you structure your closing correctly, your client will respond in the manner you want. If your client has questions, answer them, but do not be afraid to go back to the closing question.

Creating Effective PowerPoint Presentations

Let us assume you have decided to use PowerPoint slides for your business proposal presentation. PowerPoint is easy to use, if you are familiar with other Microsoft applications, because the menus and features are similar. Visual presenter applications are structured with slides that can be controlled by a mouse or remote. Each slide consists of a title and several subtitles or bullet points.

The secret to creating simple and easy-to-see PowerPoint slides is: No more than six words per bullet, six bullets per image, and six word slides in a row. In other words, each PowerPoint slide should have no more than six bullets, each containing no more than six words, and many of your slides should contain visuals rather than having all slides contain bullets. You can insert Excel spreadsheets, photos, clip art, charts, graphs, tables, and other visual elements to enhance your presentation and avoid using too many bullet slides. Consider this: Each slide should enhance your presentation and provide a powerful image. If it does not, do not use it.

Make only one major point on each slide. Ask: What does this slide say? How does it add to the case I want to make with this client? Some slides may contain only one or two words; this is acceptable if the word or words are carefully chosen and move your case along.

The most important consideration in creating your slides is this principle: The simpler, the better. Your PowerPoint slides are a visual aid, useful for guiding you through your talk and for increasing the impact of your speech. They should not detract from your words, nor should they distract the audience to the point that they cannot remember what you said.

To keep your presentation simple and easy to see:

- Stay consistent as much as possible with everything in the presentation.

- Use one font throughout the slide presentation. A sans serif font (like Arial or Tahoma) is easier to read on a screen.

- Use large type. The standard font size for titles is 44 point, and the typical size for bullet points is 28 to 32 points. Do not use *italics*, as they are difficult to read. Keep **bold** words and phrases to a minimum.

- Keep fonts and sizes consistent throughout the presentation.

- Keep transitions from slide to slide simple, avoiding "fly in" or other visually confusing transitions. In some cases, you may want to break a slide into several sections, each of which is presented separately. This is acceptable as long as you do not make the transitions too confusing.

- Use a simple, clean background. Do not use a background that fights with the words. If you are going to be in a room in which the light is dim, consider using a dark background and white fonts, for easier reading.

- Do not use all capitals; THIS IS DIFFICULT TO READ.

- Round numbers for easier reading. For example, instead of $2,341,993, use $2.3 million.

- Also avoid cents, fractions, and decimals.

- Use only one number per bullet point.

- Clearly label any visual. Make sure your readers can see the label as well as the visual.

- Skip the animation. Not only is it less professional; it is distracting for your audience.

Strategies for Increasing Effectiveness of Oral Presentations

CASE STUDY: KEVIN HOGAN

www.kevinhogan.com
Kevin@kevinhogan.com

Influential communication causes success in person and on the Web.

Influential communication includes nonverbal communication, verbal, multimedia, and simple text.

Kevin Hogan shows you how to use the mediums of communication to get to "YES!"

Kevin Hogan answers some questions on how to use body language to create a more effective proposal presentation:

Q: I am planning to use PowerPoint in my proposal presentation. Should I do that? If so, how do I use the PowerPoint slides most effectively?

A: PowerPoint can destroy as easily as it can create . . . or rather, the use misuse of PowerPoint can do this. In this case, the answer is you should use PowerPoint for about half of your presentation. You certainly don't want the machine on when

CASE STUDY: KEVIN HOGAN

you walk to the front of the room. You want to generate feelings and images in the imagination of your audience before you put your own on the screen. As soon as the PowerPoint goes up, you become less important, and you are perceived as less important. But the trade-off with effective slides with only a few words or less per slide, can work.

Q: Where should I stand in relation to the screen?

A: You want to present from stage left. That means as you look at the audience, you will always be on YOUR "left of center" side of the room when presenting your ideas and proposals. The brain science on this is extensive; this works. When the screen is darkened and you are "on," then things can change and it matters where you stand to deliver various emotional concepts, stories, and the like.

Q: How do I use eye contact to keep the attention of the audience?

A: Capture four to seven people's eyes in the audience. Communicate with those people. Don't try to look at the entire audience. You can't, and there are too many surprises out there for you if you do. Pick a few people and tell each person a short story or piece of information. Don't dart between people or scan.

Q: How do I control my movements so they don't distract the audience?

A: Keep your hands between your shoulders, above the waist and below the neck. Stage movement is a science, and it takes time learn how to block out a presentation so it sells. That's a bit advanced for this context. Keep your hands in close. Feel free to gesture, but never point with neutral or negative emotion toward your audience. You can point to someone who has won an award and you are highlighting them. You can't point at your audience and have them feel good about you in many contexts.

Q: How do I gain the attention of the owner of the company and persuade him to agree to my proposal?

A: Don't flatter the owner too much. It is very obvious and poor strategy. A gentle challenge is much better. Persuade the owner by maintaining eye contact with him more than any other individual. Respect distance between you and the owner; don't come any closer than six feet. Anything you want the owner to touch, hand it to someone else to hand to the owner; find someone she obviously likes and respects. Gain attention by telling a short story about how the owner started the

CASE STUDY: KEVIN HOGAN

business in 1988 and why she did what she did to make it successful, and now you are going to show the audience how she continues on in that tradition of achievement.

Q: Should I spend much time focusing on the rest of the audience? How do I figure out to gain the attention of each person when there are several in the audience?

A: Yes, you should focus on the rest of the audience. The owner has them there for a reason. Connect with the people who are giving you good feedback. If people are taking notes, talk to them. Talk to people who are nodding their heads, and talk to people who have pens in their hands.

Q: What are some pitfalls to avoid in giving this presentation?

A: The first is standing too close to decision makers, as I mentioned above. Second is being dressed distractingly if you are woman. That is, do you look like a man? That's bad. If you are a woman, be professional with very little, if any, jewelry. Keep your earrings simple, with small hoops, something straight that flatters but doesn't distract. For both men and women, do not chew gum; don't drink water with ice, and avoid anything that is carbonated.

There are hundreds of ways your body language can screw up a presentation. For example, don't smile any more than makes sense. Are you a woman talking to men? Then be pleasant, easygoing, certain, confident, comfortable, not abrasive or overwhelming. Don't try to be a man.

If you are a man presenting to men, avoid competitive stances and gestures. Keep your testosterone stories to yourself if you are in a mixed audience. Smile when it is appropriate.

For both genders: Don't look at the screen. A quick glance every now and then is OK, but if you get into using the screen as a crutch, you will pay a price.

Q: What are some key points you can give me to help me make this proposal successful?

A: Here are just a few:

- Ask questions as a presenter to make sure you are on the same page as the audience. Look for feedback. A lot of speakers run past feedback, like everyone in the audience putting their pens down, or seeing blank stares.

CASE STUDY: KEVIN HOGAN

• You MUST move from point to point like an actor. Actors don't pace. They move with intention. They have specific places they tell specific stories from. They deliver lines from precise locations. If you move but avoid pacing, you gain respect and attention.

• Be authentic as a speaker. Care about the company and its people. If you don't care, don't try to fake it; you will come off as counterfeit.

• Follow the feedback with your audience. If you have a 90-minute presentation and you see coffee on the tables, please give everyone a break at the 40-minute mark. If you have more than a few women in the room, make it a 10 minute break instead of five. Then start precisely on time . . . or when the owner/money maker/decision maker returns.

Here are some suggestions for enhancing the effectiveness of your presentation:

- Provide handouts so your audience can follow along and take notes. The PowerPoint application has several options for handouts. Consider printing the handouts at three per page, with lines for notes. This allows your audience to jot down questions or key points you have discussed.

- Look carefully at your graphics, particularly tables and spreadsheets. Your audience must be able to read clearly what is on the table. If they cannot, the slide will detract from your presentation. If the slide is essential to presenting your case, print it and hand it to the audience. You can show a section of an spreadsheet, but make certain it is completely readable.

- Hyperlinks (links to the Internet or other documents) can be inserted into PowerPoint slides, but be careful with using hyperlinks. Know where the hyperlink will take you (in other words, be certain it is an active link) and be certain you know how to get back. The hyperlink may open up another browser window, and if you are not aware of this, it can leave you wondering how to get back to your presentation.

- Use titles on your slides to keep your audience informed. If you have a series of slides on one point, for example, title them "Benefits – Slide 1" and so on.

- Insert video or audio to make a strong point with your audience. Be sure the sound is turned to the right volume and your video or audio is not too long.

- Photos and art can be powerful visuals. Do not hesitate to use a photo in place of words. Visuals are important in the beginning and at the closing. A great visual can provide emphasis for your "call to action."

- Be dull. Let your speaking control the audience; do not let them get so fixed on the PowerPoint slides that they are not paying attention.

- When you are presenting, stand beside the screen. Do not stand with your back to the audience. You are the presenter, and you must be seen. Sometimes it is difficult to make eye contact with your audience in a dim room with a PowerPoint presentation. You may want to turn off the data projector at the end so you can connect with the audience for your closing. Remember, the slides are supposed to help you increase your effectiveness, not do your work for you.

Using Humor to Add Interest to Your Proposal

CASE STUDY: JOHN KINDE

Humor Specialist and Keynote Speaker
Las Vegas, NV
www.humorpower.com
702-263-4363

John Kinde creates and delivers motivational programs for conventions, meetings, or workshops. His Web site (**www.humorpower.com**) includes resources for improving humor and public relations skills. John provides one-on-one coaching for people who want to improve their persuasive speaking skills and enhance their careers through improved confidence and speaking ability.

John has some tips for adding a fun touch to proposal presentations:

1. Remember the advice of "less is more." One good laugh line is far better than four jokes when two of them are just mildly funny. Pick your best line and go with it.

2. It is tricky targeting humor for an audience to which you don't belong. For example, if you are making a proposal to a law firm, and you are not a lawyer, doing lawyer jokes is risky. First, you don't have a sense for what is truly funny in someone else's profession. Second, if it is a great line, they have probably already heard it.

3. Relevant humor is very important. If you tell a joke and it has no relevant point to your proposal presentation, people will think, "So what?"

4. Poking fun at yourself is usually safe and fun. However, this technique can also be tricky if not done right. It is usually OK to make fun of your shortcomings, but avoid poking fun at your professionalism. For example, if a man looks like a professional basketball player, at 6 foot 8 inches and 240 pounds, and he was making a proposal for installing a corporate gym, he could say, "I am an expert in exercise for improved workplace performance . . . and I am a former professional jockey." It creates a funny picture. Is that joke relevant? In my opinion, yes. It gives the audience insight into your personality by

CASE STUDY: JOHN KINDE

telling them that you have a sense of humor. That is a plus in establishing a trusted business relationship. On the other hand, if a person is obviously out of shape, poking fun at that fact would be a bad idea while selling gym equipment!

5.   Avoid hot-button humor areas. Sex, body parts, bodily functions, and classic four-letter words are off limits in a business presentation. This includes innuendo; hinting at something you cannot say directly is something you always want to avoid. These hot-button areas may get a quick, easy, cheap laugh, but they lower the professionalism of your presentation. You might want to add to that list: race, religion, politics.

6.   Develop your observational humor skills. It is often the best way to get a laugh. If you can make a humorous connection with something that happened just before you spoke, or if you notice something in the room that is a good target for a joke, it will usually get big laughs because it is fresh and in the moment. This is a skill that is developed over time. At every meeting you attend, practicing using one observational humor comment near the end of the meeting.

7.   If you are serious about improving your presentations, your humor, and your ability to connect with an audience, join a Toastmasters Club (**www. toastmasters.org**). If you are not a member of a Toastmasters Club, you are missing out. It is one of the best places to exercise your speaking skills, it is affordable, and it is the perfect place to practice observational humor. Toastmasters is an international public speaking organization with over 220,000 members in 11,300 clubs in 90 countries. There is probably a Toastmasters Club in your city.

8.   Work on improving your proposal presentations with humor. It is a great investment — your audiences will like you more, listen to you more, believe you more, and buy from you more.

Dress for the Success of Your Presentation

Most businesspeople are aware of the importance of dress for making a positive impression on business prospects, and many studies have shown that something as simple as choice of dress or suit can affect the success of a proposal. This section will discuss a few ways you can improve the success of your presentation through dress and appearance.

- Dress one step above the business attire of the office where you are presenting. Many offices these days have gone to "business casual," and few men and women wear suits in the office. Wear a suit anyway. It is better to be overdressed than underdressed. A tie may be optional, but not if the men with whom you are meeting have ties on.

- Wear a conservative suit or dress.

- Keep accessories minimal. Some businesspeople object to obvious piercing (other than women's earrings). Flashy jewelry is out of place for both men and women.

- Also keep perfume or cologne to a minimum or, better yet, leave it off. Some people are allergic to some scents and you may cause a problem for someone without meaning to.

- If you are a woman, avoid heavy makeup and loud nail polish. Nothing on your person should call attention to itself. Also, women should avoid low-cut, tight, or overly feminine blouses. In this case, more clothing is best.

- Avoid offending with odors. Make sure your teeth are brushed and you use mouthwash; use a good deodorant.

- Do not forget your shoes. They should be appropriate business shoes with a polish or at least no obvious scuff marks or signs of wear. People look at you from head to toe when they first meet you. If you have a great suit and tie, but you have forgotten to polish your shoes, you may have diminished your chances of success. Women should avoid open-toed shoes unless they are very conservative.

- No gum or mints. Leave the gum outside and finish or discard the mint before you enter the presentation.

The key words for dress are:

- Inoffensive

- Inconspicuous

- Neat

- Conservative

CHAPTER 21

SALES PROPOSALS TO CUSTOMERS

Using the AIDA Format

Successful sales proposals follow a time-tested format called AIDA: Attention, Interest, Desire, Action. The AIDA principle is a good way to structure a personal appeal or to sell a product or service to a client.

A = Attention. First, the proposal must capture the reader's attention. Without getting a person's attention, you cannot sell them anything. There are several good ways to get a client's attention in a sales presentation:

- Make a surprising statement. For example, "Your company may be losing money every month — right through the roof."

- Use a statistic. For example, "Small retail businesses lose more than $35 million a year on employee theft."

- Ask a shocking question. For example, "Did you know that employee theft is the biggest reason for business failure?"

In most cases, you should "pull" the listener toward you rather than "push" the reader away from you with a scare tactic. Use the attention-getting opener to point out a client problem. Then in the rest of your sales message, describe how you can help solve that problem.

I = Interest. Create and sustain your client's interest in your business proposal by:

- Showing the client that you have a genuine concern about their problems.

- Demonstrating that you can help solve the problem, with specific examples of how you can do this. The general rule here is, "Show, do not tell." In other words, show the client you can help rather than telling the client you can help.

- Actively involving the client in the discussion of the problem and the possible solutions. If you can ask good questions and get a dialog going, you will find that most clients become engaged and interested.

D=Desire. Once you have the client's attention and she is interested in what you can do, your next job is to create a desire for your service or product to solve the client's problem. Some methods to increase desire include:

- Make the client believe the product or service will not be available long or that it will not be available at the current price. This is called the "scarcity" principle, and it is effective in causing people to act when they may not otherwise do so. Use the scarcity principle carefully, and be certain you are telling the truth about the availability or the price change. Some people are skeptical of this type of claim and they may not believe you, particularly if you or your company has used this device in the past. Make your claim of scarcity believable if you want it to be effective.

- Show the client that others believe in you and your company and your products and services. This is called "social proof," and as has been discussed elsewhere in this book, it is the most powerful and most effective method of persuasion. Use testimonials, success stories, and examples to show how others have benefited by using your product or service. Make a strong case with several good examples. The words "approval" and "benefit" should be sprinkled throughout your presentation at this point.

- Show the client how you specifically can solve his problem with the products or services you provide. Create a strong visual picture of the "after" to help the client see what success would look like. Weight loss ads do this well; use this strategy to create desire in your client.

A=Action. This is the final and most important step in the sales process. It is the "call to action" or "closing the sale." You must be able to finalize the sale by making a closing statement. Without a strong action call, you will not be able to successfully finalize the sale.

The closing must provide enough interest to keep the reader engaged and keep her reading. It must build a strong desire in the reader to want what the presenter is proposing, and it must conclude with a strong "call to action," so that the reader knows clearly what is expected. All four elements are important for a successful proposal.

CASE STUDY: CLOSING THE SALE

Information on closing sales is presented by Kelley Robertson.

Closing the sale in a business proposal is a process, not an event. It does not occur just because you have asked for a commitment or because you have presented all the features and benefits of your product or service. When a customer or prospect agrees to do business with you after reviewing your proposal, it means that you have addressed his key issues and demonstrated exactly how your solution will benefit his company. This requires strategic planning.

Effective proposals often start with an executive summary which highlights the prospect's current situation or problem and how this issue could be affecting the company. Unfortunately, too many salespeople spend too much time talking about their company, product, or service at the beginning of the proposal. The drawback with this approach is that decision-makers are extremely busy, which means they do not want to waste their time reading something that has little or no relevance to their situation. Salespeople will argue this information is critical and they need to present

CASE STUDY: CLOSING THE SALE

it to show how their solution is appropriate to the customer's situation. While this is true, it is essential to direct your initial focus on the customer and demonstrate that you have a good understanding of your prospect's issues and concerns.

Closing the sale in a proposal means positioning your solution and demonstrating exactly how your prospect will benefit by using your product or service. Far too many salespeople forget this critical element. They discuss many of the features and benefits of their solution but they fail to outline the impact of their solution on the prospect's business. The challenge is that the majority of salespeople do not discuss this with their prospect. Therefore, they cannot address it in their proposal. This approach means you have to ask thoughtful and insightful questions that most salespeople shy away from.

Closing the sale in a proposal can mean reducing the prospect's risk. Many people would rather tolerate working with a vendor who is not performing well than make a change because of their fear of the unknown. If this is a potential concern of your prospects, then you need to offer some type of reassurance or guarantee to reduce or eliminate this fear.

Closing the sale in a proposal also requires some form of action or commitment. Ending your proposal with a feeble statement such as, "If you have any questions please let us know" is not effective. It is essential that you clearly outline the next step(s) you expect from your prospect along with a time frame.

Effective proposals move the reader smoothly from one point to the next in a logical manner. If you ask your prospect enough of the right questions and position your solution in a manner that demonstrates how your solution is the best one for your prospect, and remove the risk, you increase your ability to close the sale.

©2007 Kelley Robertson. All rights reserved.

Kelley Robertson is the author of two books, including *The Secrets of Power Selling*, which helps sales professionals and businesses pinpoint what they need to do differently to improve their sales. Receive a FREE copy of "100 Ways to Increase Your Sales" by subscribing to his free newsletter, available at **www.kelleyrobertson.com**. Kelley conducts workshops and speaks regularly at sales meetings and conferences. For information on his programs, contact him at 905-633-7750 or kelley@RobertsonTrainingGroup.com.

CHAPTER 22

INTERNAL PROPOSALS

In many companies, executives at different levels are required to present proposals. This type of proposal is most often requested for a specific project within the company, and it may be solicited by the top management, or it may be unsolicited and presented by you and a few colleagues.

Here are some suggestions for improving your chances of having a proposal accepted by your boss and other top executives:

- **Talk benefits.** Describe measurable and quantifiable benefits that this proposal will bring to the company. If the benefits are intangible, try to find something you can discuss to focus your audience on benefits.

- **Appeal to ego and ambition.** If you are presenting your business proposal to the top executive, show her that the proposal will bring prestige to her and the company, or compare the foresight of this individual with the acumen of other top executives at Fortune 500 companies.

- **Talk "bottom line."** Try to show how your proposal will improve profits or reduce costs. If you cannot talk specifics, mention things such as improved employee retention or reduced turnover, both of which result in lower costs to the company.

- **Make it easy to say "yes."** Discuss any blocks and negatives, showing how you have already dealt with these or how you plan to deal with them in the future. Show that others in the company are in agreement, and ready for the change. Overcoming objectives is an important way to get someone to agree to a proposal.

- **Stay positive.** Adopt a friendly approach, talking about your feelings about the company.

- **Suggest a trial basis or pilot.** In many cases, an executive will be persuaded to accept a proposal if you propose a short-term, low-cost trial with an evaluation at the end.

CHAPTER 23

WHITE PAPERS AS PROPOSALS

A white paper is an authoritative document, written by an individual who is an expert in a specific field of study or endeavor. While not strictly a business proposal, a white paper is sometimes used as a sales document. More often, a white paper is informational in nature, used to portray an array of data and statistics in a format useful to decision makers.

White papers are written by government employees, contractors, and businesspeople. White papers are often written to explain the benefit of a course of action or a new product or service. For example, a technology company may create a white paper to tout the benefits of its new technological capabilities. Or a software company may want to inform users of new features in its latest version.

Within business proposals, white papers can be an effective means of providing additional information. White papers may also be used as a stand-alone business proposal, although in this sense, they would not strictly be considered a white paper.

To include a white paper in a business proposal, you may want to set it off at the end in an appendix. Here is a typical format for a white paper:

- Market Situation

- Problem Development

- Historical Overview

- Solution

- Benefits

CHAPTER 24

GOVERNMENT CONTRACTING PROPOSALS

Creating an RFP

You may need to write a request for proposal (RFP) or respond to one. In either case, you should be familiar with the general format for RFPs. The outline of these documents varies considerably, because each state and branch of the federal government has its own format. Here are the sections you can expect to find in most RFPs:

1. Guidelines for making a proposal to a governmental entity:

   - Schedule of events

   - Special terms and conditions

   - General information

     a. Definitions

     b. Purpose

     c. Background

     d. Payment method

2. Technical specifications

    •   Specifications (for products) or scope of work (for services)

    •   Project management

    •   Deliverables schedule

    •   Support, training, and maintenance

3. Vendor requirements

    •   Mandatory requirements

    •   Vendor qualifications and experience

    •   References and resumés

    •   Financials

4. Evaluation and reward

    •   Evaluation criteria

    •   Discussion

    •   Negotiations

Creating Proposals in Response to RFPs

Responding to a RFP takes careful attention to detail and to the specific requirements stated in the RFP. Since an RFP is written by a governmental agency, you will find they are detailed and exacting in their requirements. You cannot deviate from the outline or miss a requirement if you want a chance to be awarded the contract.

Before you begin to respond to the RFP, carefully review the document to be certain you understand it. This may take several readings, depending on the complexity of the RFP and its source (governmental entity or corporation).

One of the most important sections of an RFP is the "deliverables." These are tasks or products delivered by the customer. For example, if the project requires that your company produce 100 computers by a certain date, the computers are the deliverables. When you are reviewing an RFP to consider whether or not to submit a proposal, pay attention to the "deliverables" so you can see what is required of vendors who are successful in their proposal.

RFPs also include specific requirements or specifications that must be fulfilled. For example, in addition to producing 100 computers, you may be required to include certain software or other components.

Finally, the RFP will include a timeline with deadlines for delivery or performance. All three of these components — deliverables, specifications, and deadlines — must be addressed in your proposal.

To increase your chance of being awarded a contract as a result of an RFP, be certain that you can fulfill all of these criteria:

- You have demonstrated that you understand the requirements of the RFP.

- You have demonstrated that you can fulfill the requirements of the RFP.

- You have a clearly defined approach to creating value for the client.

- You have a competitive pricing structure for your proposal.

CHAPTER 25

BUSINESS STARTUP PROPOSALS

L ike other types of business proposals, startup proposals are sales documents, but of a different kind. Business startup proposals are a specific type of business proposal. These documents include many of the principles and formatting similarities as other business proposals, but with some differences. The typical business proposal is written to obtain a sale or to present a product or service agreement. Business startup proposals, on the other hand, are usually written to obtain financing from a bank, lender, or investor.

The business startup proposal includes many of the same elements as other business proposals:

- The startup proposal should contain an executive summary. In this case, the executive summary is useful to the banking or lending executive, or the principal in a venture capital organization, who needs to have an overview of the business, the amount requested, and the plan for paying it back.

- The startup proposal includes background information. In this case, the background section discusses the formation of the company (if it is currently in operation), the current situation, and the financial situation of the business.

- Startup proposals include detailed financial data showing the effect of the requested financing on the financial viability of the company. Most often included in the financial section are: a startup financing worksheet, cash flow and profitability statements for up to three years, and a sources and uses of funds statement showing how the requested funds will be used.

- Startup proposals include information about the people involved with the company, and details about their background and expertise.

- Startup proposals, like all other types of business proposals, are sales documents.

Unlike other types of business proposals, on the other hand:

- Startup proposals must include much more detail on financial implications of the proposal, since a banker or lender will be looking closely at these financial statements.

- Startup proposals usually do not include much background explaining the rationale for the proposal, since it is obviously a proposal to obtain money for startup.

- Startup proposals typically include information on how the business will be marketed, whereas in many other types of business proposals, marketing is not an aspect to be considered.

Here is a side-by-side comparison of the format of a startup proposals with other types of business proposals. The business plan format used is based on the format suggested by the Small Business Administration (SBA):

Startup Proposals	Other Business Proposals
Executive Summary	Executive Summary
General Company Description	Introduction and Background
Product/Service Plan	Goals and Objectives
Demographic Analysis	Methods and Tasks
Competitive Analysis	Timelines
Marketing and Promotion Plan	
Management Plan	
Operating Plan	
Financial Plan and Financial Spreadsheets	
Conclusion and Request for Funding	Conclusion
Supporting Financial Statements and Other Appendixes	Appendixes

Sections of a Startup Business Proposal

1. **Executive Summary.** In a startup proposal, the executive summary provides the reader with a short narrative describing the company and includes information on the funding needed and the expectations of the business to pay back these funds. A typical executive summary in a startup business proposal may include:

   a. A short description of the business, including location and startup date.

   b. Information on the owner or owners and the people who will be in top management positions.

   c. A statement about the type of legal structure of the company.

   d. A sentence or two describing the total funding required for startup, the form of this funding (loans, equity capital, other sources of funds) and the expectation of the business for paying back loans and distributing earnings to investors.

2. **General Company Description.** This section provides more detail on the company, its location, expected start date, type of business, and the legal form of business. While this section mirrors much of the information in the executive summary, remember that the executive summary is a stand-alone document that can be read without the rest of the business startup proposal.

3. **Product/Service Plan.** This section describes in detail the products and services sold by the company. It may include product descriptions, information on manufacturing processes or sales processes, or details of sources of products for resale. Service descriptions include information on how services are provided and to whom. Details on pricing for products and services are included, as well as distribution channels.

4. **Demographic Analysis.** For a business that sells locally, the city and location of the business is described in this section, along with population demographics, including total population, number of households, average household income level, average educational level, ethnic distribution of population, and other information specific to the products or services of the company. Areas from which expected customers will be drawn should be included. For businesses that operate regionally, nationally, or globally, a detailed description of the market segments for the company's products and services should be provided.

5. **Competitive Analysis.** The largest and most important direct competitors for the company's products and services should be described, along with their relative market share, their unique selling proposition, and an analysis of their competitive threat to the company.

6. **Marketing and Promotion Plan**. In this section, you will describe all of your marketing and promotion activities, focusing on the first year

of your business, but including possible future promotional activities. This section is important because your lender or investor will want to see how you plan to promote your business to get customers or clients on a regular basis, and to provide the income to pay back your loans or provide dividends earnings for investors.

7. **Management Plan.** Descriptions of the qualifications and experience of the individuals who are part of the business are included in this section. For all of these people, you will need to write a short resumé or biography showing how this person's education, experience, and knowledge will help make this business successful. You may also want to include more complete resumés in an appendix. The management plan is usually divided into three categories of individuals:

   a. **Owners:** These are the individuals who are making the executive decisions for the company. Include information for yourself and others who are owners or general partners, or members (for an LLC).

   b. **Employees:** Discuss what your organization structure will look like and your plans for hiring individuals. Include position descriptions for key individuals. If you already have hired employees, describe their backgrounds and how they will be of value to you and your business.

   c. **Advisors:** Your business advisors may include your company attorney, CPA, banker, and insurance agent. You may also want to include any coaches or outside business advisors who will be working with you to help get the business started. Do not forget to include your board of directors.

8. **Financial Plan and Financial Spreadsheets.** A key to acceptance of any business startup proposal is an excellent set of financial documents. Your lender or investor will want to see at least three

years of financials, to gauge the long-term viability of this startup proposal. The most important documents to include in your startup proposal are:

a. A startup spreadsheet, showing the facilities costs, equipment, supplies, initial inventory, and other costs needed to open the doors. Sometimes this spreadsheet is called a "Day One" spreadsheet. The more details you include on this worksheet, the better.

b. Income estimates on a monthly basis, by product or service category. These estimates should include reasonable estimates, not wildly optimistic ones.

c. A cash flow worksheet showing details of income by category, discounts/returns/allowances, and funds received, along with all business expenses, and net cash flow for each month and accumulated. This worksheet should be prepared to show month-by-month details for each of the first three years of the business.

d. An annual projected income statement for each of the first three years of the business. This worksheet should show net sales, expenses (including depreciation), net income before taxes, estimated taxes, and net after-tax income.

e. A sources and uses of funds statement that provides details of funding required, including working capital needed during the first few months after startup. This document should show how much you plan to contribute to the initial financing for the business, and the net needed from lenders or investors.

Many business startup proposals include appendixes with additional marketing demographics, resumés of key individuals, fees and pricing structures, and other information.

CASE STUDY: DR. JANEL VOELKER

Coastal Wellness Family Chiropractic
300 Ocean House Road
Cape Elizabeth, ME 04107
207-799-WELL
www.coastalwellnesschiro.com

Dr. Janel Voelker graduated from Palmer College of Chiropractic in February 2007 and was in her chiropractic practice working by March 15, 2007. She opened her doors to the public on April 19, 2007. This very fast work for a new healthcare practice, is due to Dr. Voelker's planning during chiropractic college, and to her effort in putting together an excellent business plan.

She began her planning process well before graduation by purchasing office and clinic equipment and doing the background research for her startup proposal. She did a lot of market research to find a community in which to practice. She and her husband were not sure what city they wanted to live in, but they did know they wanted to be on the coast; they also wanted a city where the population ratio for chiropractors was low. She focused on the state of Maine and found that Cape Elizabeth had a population of 9000 with no chiropractor. She also found that this city had an affluent population, which meant she could more easily establish a "cash" practice there.

Much of Janel's efforts in preparing her startup proposal focused on the financial aspects. Using spreadsheets she was given in class, she prepared the following documents:

1. A startup worksheet showing all of the equipment and supplies and other items she would need to open the practice.

2. A personal budget, so she could determine how much money she would need to take from the practice for personal expenses.

3. Month-by-month cash flow statements showing net collections and expenses for each of the first three years of her practice.

4. A pro-forma income statement showing net collections, business expenses (including depreciation), net income before taxes, estimated taxes, and net after-tax income. These statements were prepared for three years.

CASE STUDY: DR. JANEL VOELKER

5. Detailed expenditures for marketing and promotion activities for the first year, with monthly totals.

6. A worksheet showing estimated costs for employee pay and benefits monthly for the first year.

7. Finally, a sources and uses of funds statement showing the total amounts needed to be financed, the amounts available from her personal funds, and the amount needed from a lender.

Janel remembers reworking the financial numbers over and over as she found new information on costs and as she re-evaluated her estimates of income. When she had completed her planning process, prepared the financial statements, and written the business startup proposal, Janel began taking this document to banks requesting funds. The first bank, a large national banking institution, laughed at her and stated that no one would ever give her a loan for her new business. The second bank, a local lender, had a much more open and friendly attitude toward her, and they were willing to help.

The worst part of the process of presenting her business proposal was the pride issue. She and her husband wanted to set up the business on their own, with no need for a cosigner or a loan from family or friends. She remembers walking out of the interview with the first bank that turned her down, and thinking, "What are we going to do?" She remembers the event as a huge disappointment.

Her persistence paid off, and she did get the startup funding she needed, although it came from her family and not from a bank. But she learned valuable lessons about preparing a business startup proposal which she said has been helpful in her practice.

She also had great business role models in her parents. Growing up in a family where both of her parents owned and operated their own businesses, she saw from her parents' work the rewards of being your own boss. After she found the funding and opened her office, the biggest challenge she faced was the first few months. She remembers this as a "scary" time, when she would go to the office every day and sit and wait for patients to call or walk in the door. Her biggest challenge during this time was keeping a positive attitude about her future success.

Slowly the business improved, and she began to see a positive cash flow during her fourth month of business. She was able to take an owner's draw during her fifth

CASE STUDY: DR. JANEL VOELKER

month. Among her mistakes in startup was learning to set limits on her time. On her day off, for example, she would come into the office to see patients. She now realizes it is important to have a day to rejuvenate and focus on her personal life and growth outside the business. Janel says she has also learned to say "no" to salespeople, who, she says, will never leave you alone if you are not firm with them.

She believes there are important characteristics every small business owner must possess. First, she says, is self-motivation. You need to be able to keep yourself pumped up about your business, especially during the process of presenting your business startup proposal and during those first few months when things are not growing as fast as you imagined they would.

The second quality small business owners must possess, she believes, is passion. "If I were not passionate about helping people through chiropractic care," she says, "I would have had some difficult days getting going, but my passion has always carried me through." Finally, she believes vision is important. She says you need to be able to see yourself succeeding with your business proposal and in your business, so you can envision the potential you have to grow.

Dr. Voelker's advice to someone who is thinking of starting a new business and preparing a business startup proposal is not to get discouraged by things that seem like setbacks. For example, when she first came to town and started looking for office space for her practice, she found what seemed like the perfect location. She kept going back to the owner with new offers, all of which were rejected. Finally, she gave up on her efforts to get that office space and she found a new space which is much better. While she was initially crushed that she did not get the original space, she learned there was a better space waiting for her. Even if a big thing goes wrong, she says, there is another plan waiting for you. She believes that if you keep trying, you will succeed.

CHAPTER 26

A SUCCESS STORY: LEARNING FROM YOUR MISTAKES

Jonathan Lazar
29-11.com
jonathan@29-11.com

Twenty-Nine 11 Studios is an identity company that is located in Michigan, and works with clients across the United States. The owner, Jonathan Lazar, started his business by re-branding his father's engineering company. Since then, he has worked primarily with chiropractors to develop their brand processes.

After Twenty-Nine 11 Studios first three projects, they had 13 requests from potential clients for proposals. Of the 13 proposals presented by Twenty-Nine 11 Studios, only one was accepted and that was seven months after the fact. Jonathan found that the prospective clients were experiencing "sticker shock" when they saw the prices in the proposal, and he was not sure what to do about this issue. Although he was pricing in accordance with the work that needed to be done and his rates were significantly below those of other design firms, he found that people were not willing to accept these prices because they did not know what they were getting for the money. He realized he was doing something wrong, so he sought help. Jonathan found that several factors were standing in the way of his proposals being accepted: the proposal document itself, relationships, and value pricing.

Jonathan said the initial proposal process was not resulting in accepted proposals. The branding proposal process at Twenty-Nine 11 Studios began with a needs analysis meeting. The two primary purposes of this meeting were to determine if the company could do what the client wanted, and to see if they wanted to work with the client. The company strongly felt that they should only take on the clients they could help and with whom they could have a mutual relationship of trust and understanding. Jonathan said that after one meeting, he and his sales manager decided they would not take the client because they did not feel the relationship would work. The company has become more skilled at determining how many revisions the client will request so they can determine a price for the project that will reflect the amount of reworking that must be done.

After the meeting, which is sometimes conducted in person but is more often handled through a phone call or videoconference, Jonathan prepares his proposal. When the company first started presenting proposals, the proposal design consisted of a cover page, a complete site architecture map of the Web site Twenty-Nine 11 Studios would be designing, along with a detailed pricing proposal. One problem they discovered after delivering several proposals was that clients would turn down his proposal, and take the site architecture they had provided to another Web designer. Jonathan found he was giving away valuable up-front proprietary product to prospective clients who were not seriously interested in working with him.

Jonathan learned that his personal relationship with the client is the most important factor in getting the proposal accepted and in gaining client satisfaction. "If the relationship is not working for you (the client) or me (the service provider), we can't provide the service you want," Jonathan states. "You have to have a mutual feeling, a 'kindred spirit,'" with this client before you can work together." As a case in point, he has found that most clients prefer to work directly with him on proposals. In the beginning, he had account managers do the proposal meetings with clients, but the results were disappointing. He discovered that he was the person people wanted to talk to; they would not open up to the account managers. So he stopped having others do the proposal meetings, and he handles the meetings himself.

He also found that creating value for his company's services in the mind of the client is vital to getting a proposal price accepted. If the client values the proposal, the price is no problem. If the offering is not valued, the price will be an obstacle. But the perception of value must start first with the business person. "If you do not value your own work," Jonathan states, "you will discover that you will not be able to portray your value to your prospective clients."

Pricing is a stumbling block for many business proposal writers. After his failed attempts at proposals, Jonathan discovered that he did not believe in his prices; he had an aversion to asking so much for the work, even though he knew his company's services were worth the money he was asking. He started working with friends and offering discounts, and people began to expect more for less. He also did not want to be seen as a pushy sales type, so he hid behind his proposals.

The company's new attitude toward pricing is to first create value in the mind of the prospective client. Pricing is not discussed until the relationship is established and Twenty-Nine 11 thoroughly understands what the customer wants. In one instance, a potential customer spent much time discussing all of the possible services Twenty-Nine 11 could provide. Jonathan took this to mean the client wanted all of these services; when presented with the pricing, the client was overwhelmed. It turned out, as Jonathan listened more closely, the client wanted a few simple services. The pricing was revised and the client approved the proposal.

In Twenty-Nine 11 Studios' new pricing strategy, much thought is put into pricing for each client. The company uses different levels of pricing, based on the client's ability to clarify what is wanted, the type of work needed, and the number of revisions expected.

Today, each proposal is custom designed and written from the ground up. Although there may be common elements, each proposal is written with the specific client in mind, and most proposals take about ten hours to prepare. The company's business proposal format looks a lot different from the original. They removed the cover sheet, which they found was a waste of time and paper. They also took out the full Web site architecture completely, providing it only after the client's deposit was received. Finally, they reconfigured the pricing sheet to be clearer and more readable. The price sheet now lists all of the services that Twenty-Nine 11 Studios will do for the client, broken down into easily understood segments. The client has the option of accepting the entire proposal or any parts.

When presenting the proposal, Jonathan provides the client with a "creative summary" (an overview of the services Twenty-Nine 11 Studios will provide), and moves on to the price sheet. He concludes his brief presentation with the total price on the contract. Then he stops and waits. He says, "Whoever talks next loses." In other words, he gives his presentation and waits for a response from the client. He does not apologize or attempt to explain his pricing.

Since Jonathan has reconfigured his company value proposition, changed his mindset on pricing, and improved the proposal presentation document, every proposal he has presented has been accepted. Jonathan says his company is like the "Ritz Carlton" of branding; that is, they work hard to excel. They are open and up front with their clients, taking the time to determine exactly what clients want. They give their clients not just a brand, but a "brand process," which includes the name, tagline, colors, logo (with a font family), a Web site, and all of the other materials needed to portray the company brand (termed a "stationery system.") He says, "Everything you get from us will impress; it will never disappoint."

The company's exceptional customer service is infused into every aspect of the operations, from phone calls to written documents. Phone conversations are one example of the company's emphasis on going beyond the average. For example, at the end of every phone call with a client, employees are instructed to conclude with these words: "It was a pleasure serving you. I look forward to helping again soon." Twenty-Nine 11 Studios takes seriously the admonition to have no negatives; they avoid such terms as "don't hesitate" and "If you have concerns," believing that their positive energy has an effect on the satisfaction of their clients.

Jonathan offers some suggestions to other professionals who create and present business proposals to clients:

- Believe in and support your prices. Be comfortable in your head with what you are charging and with its value. If you do not believe in it, you cannot expect that your clients will.

- Do not hide behind your proposal. Do not apologize for the proposal or the pricing. If you have created value for your proposal in the eyes of the client, you will have no trouble getting them to agree to the proposal.

- Do not even write the proposal unless you are certain that the person is serious. If people ask about his company and services, he explains briefly what they do, by stating, "Our branding and Web services begin at $7,000." He does not call prospects; they call him. He believes people will come to him when they are ready, and that if he lays out the parameters of his work and his pricing, they will make the decision on their own and in their own time.

- Learn about the client to see if you and that person can work together productively. Say "no" to work if you feel it will cost more than your fees in energy and frustration.

- Cut back on what your proposal includes. Don't give away your proprietary work in a proposal; instead, give the prospect a brief overview with enough information to make a decision, present the pricing structure, and wait for the client to make a decision.

- Finally, spend the time up front learning about the client and his needs and wishes. The more you know about the client, the better the proposal you will be able to provide, and the more satisfied the client will be at the end of the working relationship.

CHAPTER 27

A PROPOSAL CHECKLIST

You have written the business proposal, and you are sure it is ready to send off or take to an important meeting. But before you print out 20 copies, take the time to go through your proposal, considering each item on the following checklist:

Development

1. What is your strategy in writing this proposal?

2. What specific purpose is this proposal written to address?

3. Is your objective clear to the reader?

4. What makes your proposal stand out to the reader? Why should the reader accept your proposal?

5. Does the proposal meet the specified criteria of the reader? Review the criteria.

6. Have you identified your audience and addressed the particular needs and characteristics of that audience? If there are multiple audiences, are the needs of each audience sector addressed?

7. Have you answered every one of the reader's questions? Ask someone else to read the proposal specifically for the purpose of asking this question.

Technique and Style

1. Is the proposal written clearly, using small and easy-to-understand words rather than large words?

2. Is your writing in a natural, friendly, and conversational style?

3. Is the proposal free of errors in spelling, grammar, and usage?

4. Is the proposal free of jargon? Are all technical terms described and defined clearly?

Graphics

1. Are sources cited for all graphics?

2. Are titles and descriptions for all graphics clear and helpful to the reader?

3. Are all graphics self-explanatory?

4. Does each graphic add to the proposal and provide added meaning that enhances the proposal?

Format and Organization

1. Is the executive summary written so it can stand on its own, explaining all of the major points of the proposal completely?

2. Does the organization of the proposal flow logically from one subject to another? Is there a logical order to the proposal?

3. Is there enough support for the conclusion? Did you use the best references available? Are the references adequate to make the case being presented in this proposal?

4. Did you provide an adequate amount of detail to explain key concepts?

5. Did you use definition and description to enhance the proposal?

RESOURCES

The Art of Speed Reading People: How to Size People Up and Speak Their Language. Paul D. Tieger, Barbara Barron-Tieger (Little, Brown & Co., 1999).

Business Plan in a Day: Get It Done Right, Get It Done Fast! Rhonda Abrams (The Planning Shop, 2005).

Business Plans For Dummies. Paul Tiffany and Steven D. Pearson (For Dummies, 2004).

The Elements of Style, 4th Edition. William Strunk Jr., E. B. White, Roger Angell (Allyn & Bacon, 1999).

The Business Style Handbook: An A-to-Z Guide for Writing on the Job with Tips from Communications Experts at the Fortune 500. Helen Cunningham, Brenda Greene (McGraw-Hill, 2002).

Excel 2007 For Dummies. Greg Harvey, Ph.D. (For Dummies, 2006).

Getting to Yes: Negotiating Agreement Without Giving In. Roger Fisher, William Ury, Bruce Patton (Penguin, 1991).

Handbook for Writing Proposals. Robert J. Hamper, L. Sue Baugh (NTC Business Books, 1995).

Influence: The Psychology of Persuasion. Robert D. Cialdini (Collins, 2006).

The Little Red Writing Book: 20 Powerful Principles of Structure, Style, & Readability. Brandon Royal (Writers Digest Books, 2007).

The One-Page Proposal. Patrick G. Riley (Collins, 2002).

Powerful Proposals: How to Give Your Business the Winning Edge. David G. Pugh, Terry R. Bacon (Amacom, 2005).

PowerPoint 2007 For Dummies. Doug Lowe (For Dummies, 2006).

The Science of Influence: How to Get Anyone to Say "Yes" in 8 Minutes or Less! Kevin Hogan (Wiley, 2004).

Selling: Powerful New Strategies for Sales Success. Kevin Hogan, Dave Lakhani, Gary May, and Eliot Hoppe (Network 3000 Publishing, 2007).

Writing Winning Business Proposals. Richard C. Freed, Shervin Freed, Joe Romano (McGraw-Hill, 2003).

AUTHOR BIOGRAPHY

D r. Jean Murray has been assisting small business owners for more than 27 years. Dr. Murray has an MBA and a Ph.D. in business management with an emphasis on entrepreneurship, and expertise in marketing, financial planning, and business plan preparation. She has owned and operated two successful businesses and has counseled many students and graduates with startup plans.

Dr. Murray has published several business startup books for professionals, including healthcare providers and freelance writers. Her Web site is **www. thethrivingwriter.com.**

INDEX